ENTICEMENTS

ENTICEMENTS
How to Look Fabulous in Lingerie
by Bill Tice
with Sheila Weller

Fashion Photographs by Rebecca Blake

Macmillan Publishing Company • New York
Collier Macmillan Publishers • London

Macmillan Publishing Company
866 Third Avenue, New York, N.Y. 10022
Collier Macmillan Canada, Inc.

Library of Congress Cataloging-in-Publication Data

Tice, Bill.
    Enticements: how to look fabulous in lingerie.

    1. Lingerie.   I. Weller, Sheila.   II. Blake,
Rebecca, 1949–   .   III. Title.
TT670.T53   1985   646'.34   85-13643
    ISBN 0-02-618600-4

Macmillan books are available at special discounts for bulk
purchases for sales promotions, premiums, fund-raising,
or educational use. For details, contact:
            Special Sales Director
            Macmillan Publishing Company
            866 Third Avenue
            New York, N.Y. 10022
10 9 8 7 6 5 4 3 2 1

Printed in the United States of America

To all the glamorous women whom I've learned from, helped and delighted in over the years. And to the retailers, salespeople and fashion press who have believed in my clothes and my concept since their inception.

Fashion Photographs by Rebecca Blake
Illustrations by Barbara Fox
Art Direction by Bruce Bloch
Executive Producer—Elaine Korn

CONTENTS

Acknowledgments

Still Life Photographs—Jung Lee

Head-to-Heel Sketches—Kathleen Usherwood

Fashion and Interior Styling—Ross Burman

Hair Design—Terry Foster

Make-up Artist—Gareth Green

Book Cover Makeup—Michael Reimer

Models—Carrie Nygren, Kathryn Redding, Charlotte, Drew Coburn, Paula Hamilton, Patty Owen, Gail Elliott, Vanessa Angel, Duke Lyskin, Inger, Alison Beck, Joan Severance, Deloris Henderson

Model Agencies—Elite, Ford, Wilhelmina, Zoli, Faces

Hand Model—Debra Secunda

Satin Sheets and Pillows—Emma Tirador

Floral Design—Burton Braff, Tony Lee for Lior Flowers

The Metropolitan Museum of Art, The Costume Institute

Shoes—Susan Bennis/Warren Edwards, Giovanna, Maud Frizon, Mary Beth at Ibiza, La Marca

Jewelry—Fred Leighton, Wendy Gell, Patricia Von Musulin, Bill Schiffer, Cec "Le Page" at Fragments, Ross Madole at Judith Feldman, Robert Lee Morris at Artwear, Shibatta at Artwear, Kenneth Jay Lane, Byzantium/Marc Davis at Judith Feldman

Furniture/Props—M & M Showroom, Muriel Karasik, Joia Interiors, Niedermaier, Furniture of the Twentieth Century, Vojtech Blau, Alan Moss, Christofle Silver, Lalique, Mikasa, Mood Indigo, D. F. Sanders & Co., Pratesi, Van de Lune/Wax Paper, Sentimento, Back in Black, Rubicon, A.C.C.— American Cut Crystal, Saxony Carpets, Diane Love, Pillow Finery, Lee Jofa Fabrics, Quadrille Fabrics, Yves Gonnet Fabrics, Francoise Nunnalle, John Robert Moore II

Masseuse—Paula O'Gorman

Production Assistant—Ron Haviv

A Very Special Thanks to Kathleen Usherwood, Lynn O'Donnell, Ferne Kadish, Elaine Markson, Melinda Corey, Arlene Friedman, Barbara Greenberg, Emma Tirador, Cindy Erbe, Carol McPherson

Introduction

What Is Enticement?

E nticement. Just say the word. There's an energy to it. An electricity. A charge.

Enticement. Three staccato syllables, like three quickenings of the pulse . . . or beats of the heart.

Enticement. The apple in Eve's sinuously outstretched hand. The fan fluttering against Marie Antoinette's bosom in her dazzling Versailles salon. The subtly inviting twirl of the Edwardian maiden's parasol.

How alive with magic and power, even to us today, those fabulous gestures are!

"To entice," Webster's Dictionary says, "is to set afire . . . to excite . . . to tempt, allure. . . ."

3

<u>Enticement.</u> Having lived with the second syllable of that word as my last name all my life, I have a special feeling for that magic, that power. And having spent all my working years designing clothes to help today's women achieve that very magic and power, I think I know where it all begins and what <u>enticement</u> means—not for those fabled historical women (wonderful though they were) but in the lives of real women today.

The act of enticement today is a woman's gesture to herself to call forth the other side of her moon . . . to transform herself to the nighttime glamour and fantasy that contrast with and reward her daytime self.

Enticement begins when a woman finds and cultivates what I call her Best Intimate Self: the unique sensuality available to her when the cares of the day are over . . . and the clothes of the day are, too. Now she is most purely and intensely in her own heart, her own feelings, her own skin.

With the right clothes and a little imagination and know-how, she can transport herself—and her husband or lover—out of the ordinariness of the day and into a more heightened sphere of intimacy. And whether she wants rapture and passion from these intimate hours or simple relaxation, she has learned how to create the mood that will give her just that.

Now that's enormous power.

Enticement involves a woman's power to enchant and intrigue—but not manipulatively or selfishly. And not because she has nothing else to do or nothing more on her mind. Bored women bore others. Instead, enticement depends on a vitality of spirit, a busyness of life—all splashed fresh and given great new meaning by the kind of replenishing attention a woman can only give herself.

Enticement begins with a woman caring enough about herself to care for herself well—and then to radiate that care onto others. It's another way—a more glamorous way—of saying self-esteem.

Webster's ends the definition by saying that to entice is "to attract by offering hope of pleasure and reward." When we think of those classic images of enticement—Eve and the apple . . . Marie Antoinette and the fan . . . the Edwardian maid and her parasol—we think of the receiver of that pleasure and reward as being a man.

That hasn't changed, but something has been added: A large part of the pleasure and reward of enticement—this modern enticement I'm talking about—goes to the woman herself.

I want you to have that pleasure, that reward.

Experience it! Learn from it! Delight in it!

Chapter One

Looking Beautiful in Bed

Secrets of a Lingerie Fitting Room

As women bare their bodies, they also bare their souls.

I should know. From the day I first started designing a whole new kind of sensual at-home wardrobe for the American woman (designs for which I would eventually win the Coty Award, the fashion industry's Oscar), I've spent hundreds of hours in lingerie fitting rooms all over the country, watching intricate changes take place in women's self-images as they make changes in their intimate clothes.

I've helped women across the country kick the dull matched-pink-peignoir-set habit and move into marvelously exotic caftans, djellabas and one-shoulder togas. I've guided college girls in Fort Lauderdale from nights spent in T-shirts bearing the names of their favorite rock bands to their first satin chemises and slinky floor-length gowns. I've watched harried mothers of three in Seattle suddenly get a whole new—glamorous—sense of themselves in printed strapless sarongs.

I've even heard a room full of sophisticated Manhattan women, of every possible age and in every stage of undress, shriek in unison through the curtains of the Saks Fifth Avenue dressing room as the lights went out in the great New York City blackout of 1966. (Talk about intimacy!)

As different as all these women have been, almost all of them turned to me with one form or another of the same half-request, half-confession:

"I want to look beautiful in bed! . . . And before bed, and after bed, and while I'm at home. I want to look beautiful for intimacy."

There are other confessions, too, that come before and after that main one. "I want to put the spark back in my marriage." Or, "I'm a lawyer, and all day I wear tight skirts, tight hose, snug suit jackets while I speak corporate jargon. When I come home I want to relax, be comfortable, look feminine."

Then there are women who say, "I've just had my fiftieth birthday. . . ." Or, "I've just had surgery." Or, "I've just been divorced."

But not all the women who confide in me are looking for lingerie to lift their spirits against the sobering events in their lives. Many more want their sleepwear and at-home wear to radiate and celebrate the good that's been happening to them. "I've just lost ten pounds!" and "Look at this face-lift! I feel fifteen years younger!" and "I just won the lead in a new Broadway show!" Or

"I've just had a baby and I've never felt sexier!"

Then there's my favorite: "Help me find something <u>fabulous</u>, fast! I think I've just fallen in love."

These women know that I love making women look romantic and glamorous in their intimate hours—that I understand, as they soon do, that what you wear with those you love, when only they will see you, makes a big difference in the loving.

Intimate-hours clothes are capable of creating a mood, an ambience, an emotional environment as heady and total as any created on stage or screen. No other clothes are so strongly evocative. No other clothes have such power to compel and delight and persuade, to soothe and intrigue and provoke.

How did I learn this?

When I was growing up in a small town in Indiana, I used to go to the local movie theater every Saturday. The white-picket-fence world that I lived in, as wonderful as it was, would give way in a flash to some glamorous big-city boudoir as I inched my way in the dark to my seat.

There, larger than life, was Audrey Hepburn in an elegant Empire-style dress . . . Elizabeth Taylor in a creamy silk slip . . . Leslie Caron in a Belle Epoque camisole . . . Lana Turner in turban and harem pants. These women lived in a sumptuous emotional world where a man's heart could sink or a commonwealth crumble when a subtly draped shoulder was turned the right way.

Those clothes spoke a silent language fantastically foreign to the one I heard and spoke every day.

I was infatuated with that language.

(I don't think it's a coincidence that many of America's top designers of glamorous women's clothes—Halston, Bill Blass, Norman Norell—grew up in Indiana, too.)

The magic of that day-to-night flash transformation never left me. I learned to create it myself. Today when I visit the stores and departments that feature my clothes, I'm able to watch the women who walk in with the same eyes I took to my hometown matinee. I'll see a customer, not know anything about her life except what I can quickly deduce from her day clothes and hairstyle and manner, and in an instant I see her transformed into what I call

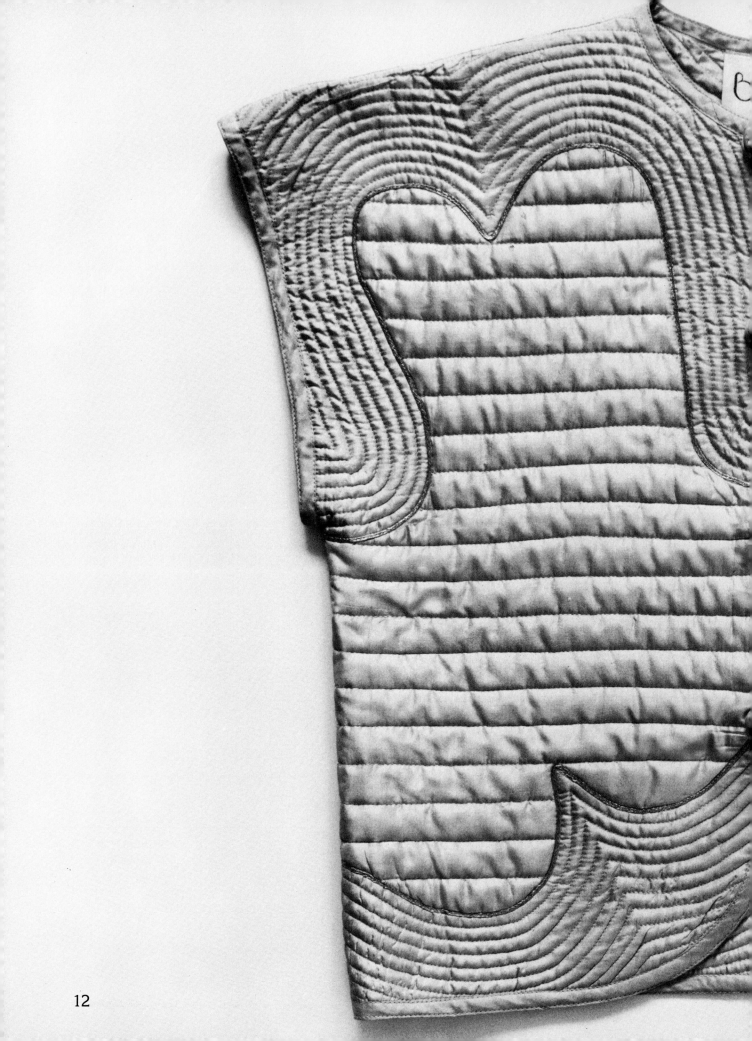

Jacket, The Costume Institute, The Metropolitan Museum of Art, 1982

her Best Intimate Self. One long, appraising glance and I've got it: the color, the shape, the mood, the line—the look.

But I'm not always successful in convincing the woman that what I see for her is best.

A Tale of Women

I'll never forget the time in I. Magnin's, a Los Angeles specialty store, when a famous man's wife and his mistress, whose identities were hardly unknown to each other, happened to be shopping for lingerie at the same time. The salespeople were doing a mad dash trying to keep each from finding out that the other was there: rushing an armful of gowns into the wife's fitting room to keep her busy inside just as the mistress was walking to the large central mirrors; then whisking her back into her curtained cubicle with a half-dozen "marvelous little numbers that are you!" just as the wife stepped out for her turn.

As I stood there watching the clothes rods being piled up with panné velvet and silk charmeuse, I noticed that everything the salespeople were selecting for the wife was modest and sweet, while the gowns for the mistress were sensual and revealing.

"Well . . . why not?" I thought, and I criss-crossed a pair of hangers from room to room.

"This is boring!" came the mistress's shout moments later.

"I can't wear this!" protested the wife.

Thank God for the muffling provided by fitting-room carpets; the women didn't recognize each other's voices.

They did know their own minds, which is all to the good.

But then again, the man still has a mistress as well as a wife.

I'm writing this book for the woman who doesn't quite know what looks best on her in bed but would like to find out. And for the woman who is willing to lay aside those safe, familiar styles she's always relied on in order to be guided to a flattering break-through intimate look that might actually change her life.

And I'm writing this book for the woman who demands a wholeness in her intimacy—a woman who doesn't want to compromise either on the way she looks when she goes to bed . . . or on the way she's loved by the man she goes there with.

I think that woman is most women.

I think that woman is you.

And if it is, I'm going to teach you how to see (and develop, and enjoy, and extend) your Best Intimate Self so that you can do it all for yourself.

Now, let's take a quick tour of the world I found myself in when I first started designing women's intimate wear, not all that many years yet a whole social lifetime ago; a world I call . . . Miss Lucy's Pink Tricot Finishing School.

Let me first of all say that today there are many marvelous, with-it lingerie saleswomen who know and love and radiate fashion. But the lingerie departments were the last to get this new breed. There's also still—and bless her heart—Miss Lucy.

You've met Miss Lucy. Perhaps she sold you your first brassiere, the straps of which she pulled briskly through what seemed to be twenty plastic adjustment notches as her charm bracelets clanked on the glass countertop. "You'll be wanting neutrals," she told you, taking two from the white box, one from the beige, one from the cream, all stiff and banded and boned.

Foundations were just so . . . <u>formidable</u> back then.

And of formidability, Miss Lucy was queen.

She always dressed in a simple but good black dress and a single strand of pearls. Her harlequin glasses were suspended from a chain around her neck (and when she peered through them hard during inventory, young sales trainees were known to wilt). Half her earthly belongings, it seemed—her lunch, her mail, her antacid tablets, the shoes she wore on the bus ride home (even more sensible than the shoes she wore on the floor)—were packed into a big black pocketbook that spent eight hours a day cleavaged between the Maidenform 34As and the Vassarette 34Bs.

Miss Lucy always told you, "Only one to a fitting room," and "Put the paper panties on first, dear," and "That little gown has a matching robe." She could match you <u>forever</u> . . . in peach on peach or mauve on mauve or rose on rose.

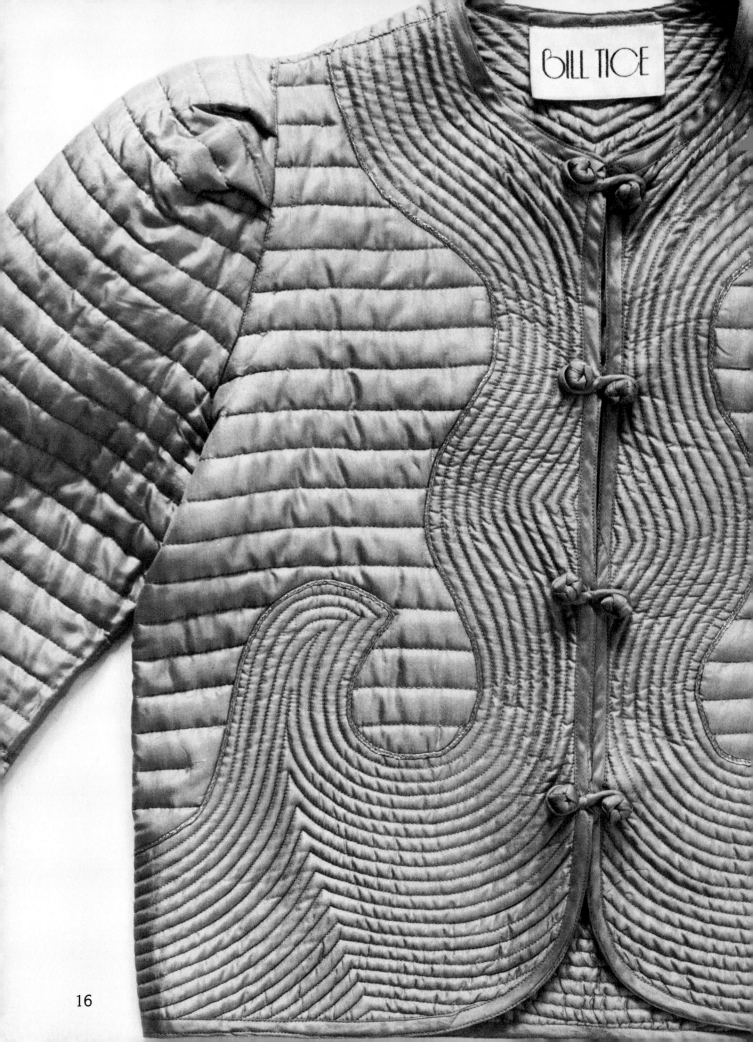

16

Jacket-Pant, The Costume Institute,
The Metropolitan Museum of Art, 1982

The image of boudoir glamour that Miss Lucy's department was selling was that of Loretta Young twirling through her open doors. As beautiful as that was for her, the reality always fell a bit short for everyone else. I'd see women stumbling out of those fitting rooms in enough feathers to fill a comforter . . . or dragging so much tricot behind them, I could swear they'd need two small train bearers just to get downstairs in the morning to make their families French toast. The alternative was high-necked flannelette that made a woman look like Little Orphan Annie.

Into this world I came in the middle sixties, ready to change everything and to help create—the great American loungewear revolution.

I started out to be a ready-to-wear designer, when a mentor of mine said, "Couture is where the good ideas have <u>always</u> been. Go to where they need to be."

That was Miss Lucy's department, all right, plus the even more neglected specialty of the soft, around-the-house clothes called loungewear.

These were "replacement" businesses, meaning customers would buy a new robe only when the old one wore out. I wanted to make them "impulse" businesses, meaning customers buy because they love what they see.

The floor displays in intimate-apparel departments were deadly dull. Everything was on a rounder—a circular display rack—so all a browsing customer could see was sleeves. (Ever wonder why so many boring gowns had such colorful sleeves?) That approach just <u>had</u> to go.

And fit, for the most part, was dreadful. Everything was oversize. Armholes went on forever. Gowns just hung from the shoulders, as if they'd been designed for hangers, not women's bodies. I wanted to change that, too, even if it meant fighting the manufacturers. (It did.)

Mostly I saw that something important was happening: All over the country, in three different but overlapping ways, American women were embarking on an entirely new style of life—and they couldn't find beautiful clothes for it!

1. There was a sudden big population shift to the Sunbelt, where people live bedroom-to-kitchen-to-pool-to-neighbor's-patio lives. Women there needed beautiful clothes to bridge the gap between indoor and outdoor, public and private. They didn't have them.

2. An increased number of women entered the work force and established real careers. Everywhere, especially in the competitive big cities, they suited up crisply by day. They came back home at dusk yearning for the feminine, glamorous equivalent of the businessman's slippers and pipe. Where <u>were</u> such soft, sensual, stress-shedding clothes?

3. Prices for women's clothes shot up just as casual living was replacing the old formal social schedules. An upper-middle-class woman could count on only occasional black-tie parties instead of her mother's steady stream. She wanted to look great for those events. But break the bank for a dress that would go out of style after three wearings? There <u>had</u> to be a better way.

I went to work to answer all these needs.

I aimed at <u>practical glamour:</u> all-season colors and fabrics; shapes—like my popular pyramidic float, that could be worn front or back; elegant reversibles; lightweight jackets that could double as evening wear; bright, stand-

out colors—jade, coral, cobalt, Chinese red—to get the blood rushing after all those years of timid pastels. Look-at-me, touch-me, feels-great-on-me clothes that could withstand all those promises made good on, that could go right from the suitcase, or washer and dryer, and over the head.

I made clothes that suggested the female body without being tacky or obvious. And sometimes I made a few that went a bit further than that. (I've always believed that every woman should own one smashing classy-tarty number. Just as every Lady of the Evening should have one floor-length Florence Nightingale in pure, pure white.)

I've had fun creating these clothes. I've taken ideas from my travels all over the world—and from the ancient Greeks and Egyptians, from Edwardian parlors and twenties speakeasies; from the color and sheen of precious stones and the wheat fields of my youth. I'd like to share the suggestions I've received from women all over the world, some of whom have been on the Best Dressed List—Dina Merrill, Barbara de Portago Grant, Nancy Kissinger, Joanna Carson, Betsy Bloomingdale, Diahann Carroll, Candice Bergen, Jaclyn Smith and Princess Michael of Kent—whose secrets of successful intimate dressing and intimate life are peppered throughout this book.

But most of my best ideas—such as the float—have come to me in dreams.

When I design, I always make sure that beauty and fantasy never get in the way of women's lives . . . and that women's lives never get in the way of their need for beauty and fantasy, either.

That balance—that totality—is much easier to achieve than you might think; you can have what's on the movie screen <u>and</u> what's in the world outside the theater, all in one day, all in one life.

Not quite convinced?

You will be when you finish this book.

Ready to start?

I thought so. Because all around me, all of a sudden, I see a whole new sense of feminine glamour starting right now.

Something is happening.

Just look at television: At night Joan Collins and Linda Evans are plotting corporate moves in beautiful, feminine lingerie. By day soap-opera stars are going to bed with each other's husbands and recovering from surgery in beautiful feminine lingerie.

And on the cable music station MTV, leggy young girls who just yesterday might have thought charmeuse was the name of a new Motown group are hopping on the backs of motorcycles and riding off into the sunset in beautiful, feminine lingerie.

Television is in the business of feeding back to us what we want to look like. What women want to look like now is feminine and beautiful.

And I don't think men would put up too much of a fight over that.

When dressed-for-success women come into intimate-apparel departments today, they're like kids in a candy store. "I can't find this romantic look anywhere else!" I've heard them say.

These women radiate competence, efficiency, power, shrewdness and authority in their daytime appearances. They love that part of themselves. They've soared with that part of themselves.

And they finally know that nothing's going to take that part away.

So now they can get on with the other part, too: the passion and languor, the Eros and pampering, the fantasy play. These women know what others are just finding out: You have an Intimate Self. And now that it's not your only self, isn't it fun to indulge it creatively!

When you look at the history of lingerie, you begin to understand that throughout time, in almost every part of the globe, everything women wore closest to their skin had to do with luring or fending off men; with churning out babies for the next bunch of wars or not churning them out because there wasn't the time or the food for them.

Lingerie was either a covering up for self-defense or a prettification of the fact that the wearer was living a life over which she had no control.

That seems shocking to us now. And sad.

Sure, a few cheeky aristocratic ladies got to do mad things with underclothes just for the fun of it, but how many of these women were there? Not very many.

This is the first time that sleepwear and loungewear are being chosen and worn by a majority of women for themselves. They really like how it looks and feels and they want to wear it.

Of course, it doesn't hurt that these women are also at the same time pleasing men. But pleasing men is a marvelous <u>bonus</u> now, not a desperate, hard-and-fast reason.

I think women want to wear beautiful lingerie again now because the bed and the home have finally become places of pleasure and choice and release for women (whether those women are stockbrokers or homemakers), not of service and duty and control.

And wearing beautiful lingerie again means . . . so long, locker-room look!

It was cute for a while, taking your gym clothes into the bedroom. It was part of your delight with your strength and your firmness and fitness. But now that you've <u>got</u> that better body, why not display it in the really sparkling clothes that are worthy of all the work you did getting it there?

The men's look in underwear might be right for certain times. But there *are* styles that more elegantly show off a woman's unique proportions and assets.

Clothes for the maintenance of the body are different from clothes for the relishment of the body. It's hard to inspire the second when you're all dressed up for the first.

A woman tennis champ, one of those marvelous tawny blondes with muscular legs and a purposeful spring to her step, recently came into Bonwit Teller in Palm Beach, where I was doing a personal appearance. She was wearing her little white tennis dress and her wristband; she left with eight of the most luscious, languorous gowns I've ever made.

"The locker room is a nice place to visit," she said. "But I don't live there."

And while we're bidding farewells, let's also finally say: good riddance, anorexia!

You <u>can</u> be too thin.

(Too rich, I'm not sure. I'm still working on that one.)

But overarticulated rib cages are really not all they're cracked up to be. And the lean and hungry look wasn't meant for all women. It wasn't even meant for most.

Women, by nature, are rounded. They have curves and cushions and padding—shelter zones against the bruises their unborn babies might suffer

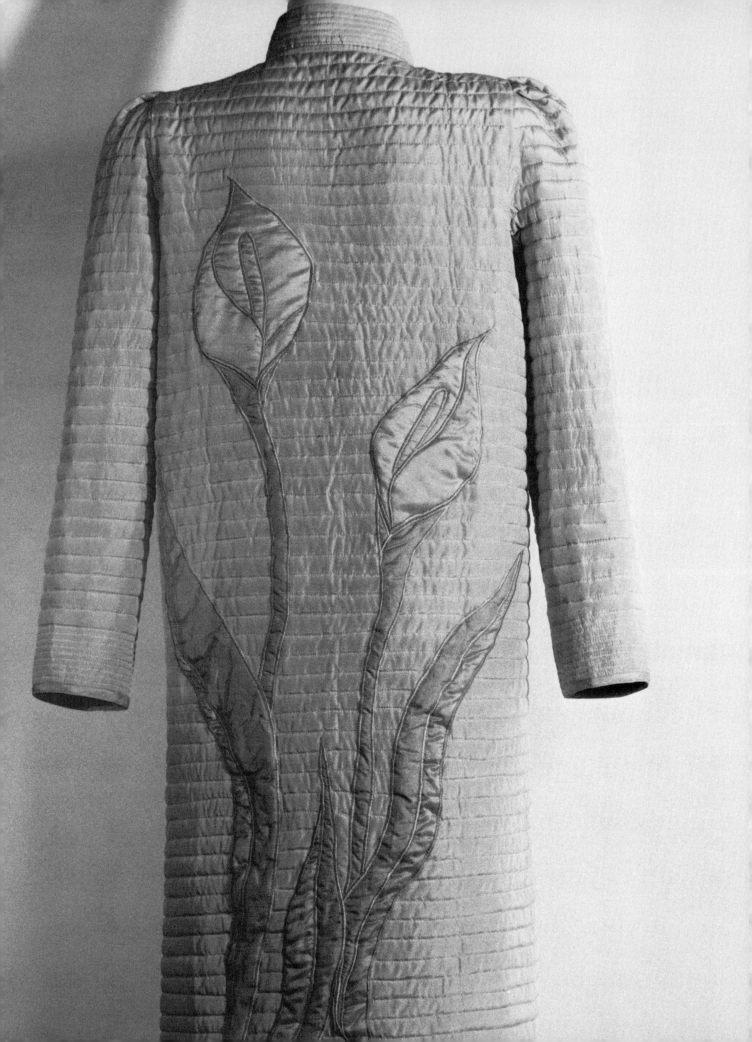

and, some poets have said, against life's more elusive sharp angles and jabs. The average woman who wasn't born to be reed slim—the woman with a little volume and fullness—got better appreciation in ages past than she does in our diet conscious culture today.

That's a shame.

But I think we're beginning to move away from that, too.

As women grow to like and trust themselves more, so do they come to like and trust their natural, God-given bodies. And as both sexes become more comfortable accepting a woman's professional strength and emotional firmness, perhaps we can also grow more comfortable accepting that same woman's physical softness and roundness.

The rounded woman wears loungewear extremely well. Intimate clothes are often loose. They fall away from the body. Voluptuous curves are softened by these clothes—as they should be in other clothes, and in other eyes, too. The wearer is not made to feel like she's stuffed into a sausage skin, not made to feel self-conscious.

And self-consciousness, uncertainty and hesitation are the biggest barriers of all. Women of all ages and body types are always asking me, "I can't wear this . . . can I?" as they point to a gown they think is delicious but the likes of which they've never worn before. They are poised on the brink of a breakthrough. They have always regarded their bed- and at-home wear as some invisible, doesn't-matter wardrobe. Now they see that it can be much more.

They've dangled their toes in the water. But they can't quite take the plunge into the pool.

Not alone, at least.

So come on! Put the tank top back in the gym locker. Throw out the old-faithful flannel pajamas. Take back that little sweet-sixteen-pink gown you just bought, in its box, to Miss Lucy and (forgive her her frown if you've already scrunched up the sales slip) just tell her to credit your charge.

Come with me. We'll get you a whole new intimate wardrobe, a whole new environment for intimacy, a whole new—and marvelous—delight and power in your Intimate Self.

Let's start with the clothes that change the mood that change the person—you—into a woman of enticement.

Chapter Two

Change Your Clothes . . .
Change Your Mood!

I always say: When you change your clothes, you change your mood. And believe me, that was never so true as when I brought a little enticement to the Tundra.

When the people from Norstrom's, a West Coast specialty store, called and invited me to become the first American designer to do a full-scale fashion show in Alaska, I thought it would be a great kick. I pictured a team of huskies bearing each of the sixteen pieces of matched luggage that would hold my collection, and me at the helm, like Nanook of the North!

And yet . . . my clothes first made their mark in the Sunbelt, not at the polar ice cap. I couldn't help but wonder: Why me?

I got my answer in the form of a down-coated woman who rushed over when she heard me being addressed by an airlines official in the VIP lounge of the Anchorage airport.

"You're Bill Tice!" she exclaimed. "We love you in Nome!" (Love me? . . . much less know me?) "Your clothes are a godsend! They save us from cabin fever!"

And so I began to understand: It was the very unlikeliness of my clothes in a place like Alaska that made them so important to the women there. These women (not to mention their husbands!) are starved for a whole different—sensual, fantasy—self at night. In a land where it stays light until ten P.M. half of the year and gets dark at four the other half, they have to work harder to achieve the dramatic mood of evening at the time that their inner clock, not the sky, says that mood should appear. And in a place where nature is so rustic and dominant—the endless white snow in winter, the dark green and brown trees—flashes of wonderfully improbable hues (lacquer red! turquoise! canary!) can hoist the physical self and the spirit up from the overwhelming landscape.

These women needed my intimate clothes to help keep their mental health!

So I set out to put on a marvelous show at Norstrom's: bright colors, sensuous music, a specially designed set that would reflect all the colors in the clothes.

It's forty minutes to showtime. The gowns are brought up from pressing; the microphones are being tested; the audience is having cocktails at a special reception.

And my star model—Number 25—calls in sick!

I have thirty-nine—no; now thirty-eight—minutes to find, hire, dress, groom and train a replacement. So I grab the fashion director by the hand and we embark on a hysterical flight through the store.

A young woman, a file clerk from across the street, is walking into the store's coffee shop. She's got on a hennaed fright wig, running shoes, tight jeans, a sloppy T-shirt—but her face is to die over.

"Quick! Grab her! I'll hold the elevator!" I tell the fashion director.

The fashion director nearly withers in disbelief.

"That's our new Number twenty-five," I say. "You've got to take 'em as you find 'em . . . <u>Then</u> you work the magic."

I pull off the woman's fright wig—and the pink plastic rollers underneath; scrub off her old makeup and redo her face; slick her hair into a classic chignon; take a deep breath as I throw a pale peach silk gown and ostrich-feather jacket over her mirrored fitting-room door . . .

And let out that breath as she emerges: transformed.

The pale peach is magnificent against her café-au-lait skin. Seeing this has sparked some inner change in her. Straight, calm, poised, she saunters—unrehearsed, mind you—out to the runway as if to the manor born.

Only after the show do I remember to call the manager of the office across the street to explain his file clerk's rather long coffee break.

You see, I had forgotten that she was a file clerk.

And <u>she</u> had forgotten that she was a file clerk.

And the women in the audience watching—and imagining themselves in—those clothes would never have guessed.

She became, for that magical hour, the pampered and glamorous goddess of a woman that the clothes she wore made her move like, and feel like, and be.

"Honey," I said, "you went out a chorus girl and came back a star!"

So you see, clothes do have a phenomenal power to change your self-image and your mood.

But that power needn't be linked to a fabulous quirk of fate, as it was with that girl. No; the mood-changing power of clothes is yours to harness and control—and use. You do that every day in your public life. Why not start doing it in your private life, too?

It all starts with the understanding that . . . your life is divided into six distinct mood zones that range from the most public to the most intimate, the most on guard and official to the most at ease and informal, the most aggressive and defensive to the most receptive, mutual and vulnerable (in the best sense of the word).

I visualize them as six concentric circles, from farthest from to closest to your inner self, your skin.

In Mood Zone 6, you are your <u>Public Working Self</u>.
In Mood Zone 5, you are your <u>Public Weekend Self</u>.
In Mood Zone 4, you are your <u>Public Evening Self</u>.
In Mood Zone 3, you are your <u>Private Party Self</u>.
In Mood Zone 2, you are your <u>Intimate Self</u>.
In Mood Zone 1, you are your <u>Bedroom Self</u> (your <u>best</u> Bedroom Self, when I get through with you!).

You breathe, sit, move, think, react and relate differently in each of these mood zones, as each of these selves. And you dress accordingly—or at least you should.

When you are your Public Working Self in Mood Zone 6, you're "on." The words that describe the clothing you wear, and the posture that clothing encourages, describe your mood and priorities as well: You're <u>girded</u> and <u>pressured</u>—by bra strap, slip strap, panty girdle, fitted suit jacket, watch strap, high-heeled shoes, cuffed and high-collared blouse . . . just as you're psychically girded against self-doubt and fear and pressured by the challenge of your task.

The style of your clothes is <u>tailored</u> and <u>ordered</u>, as is your presentation. For the most part, the fabrics are either <u>crisp</u> or <u>formidable</u>, like your attitude.

"Look. Admire. But don't touch," these clothes say.

When you're your Public Weekend Self, in Mood Zone 5, you're no longer working, but you're still doing: errands, shopping, seeing friends—in and out of home, street, car. The clothes you wear—casual styles, fabrics and cuts that allow for more movement and informal sitting, looser or flatter shoes, probably less foundations—allow you to strike the balance physically that you are striking emotionally, between accessibility and action.

"I'm approachable," your clothes say, "but I'm still on."

Now, moving from day to night . . .

In Mood Zone 4, as your Public Evening Self, you're at the theater, a restaurant, a nightclub, a charity ball. You're wearing more elegant, formal fabrics—velvet, silk jacquard, heavy satin or silk. You're flaunting your style, but you're still in public, so you can't flaunt your self. Your image is dazzling, chic, glamorous . . . but your body language is poised, invulnerable, controlled.

"Delight in me visually but keep your distance," these clothes say.

Now, moving from public to private, which is where my clothes come in . . .

In Mood Zone 3 you're your Private Party Self. Again, you're dressed dramatically for evening—but this time you're out of the public eye and in a more intimate context and mood: at a dinner party (often by candlelight and often your own), a garden or pool party, a country-club dance, an exclusive opening or reception. You feel shielded from the outside world, safe with "your own."

The clothes you wear now have softer lines, are of more sensual fabrics and frequently require fewer foundations—all of this reflecting your greater ease of movement and feeling.

"Look. Enjoy. Come a little bit closer," these clothes say.

In Mood Zone 2, as your Intimate Self, you're home free, in fact and in spirit—spontaneous, guard down, relaxed. You've pulled the curtain on a tough, ordered, demanding day and are entering, with family and maybe a few close friends, the restful, replenishing state of ease.

Though you may have tasks, they are nurturing ones: cooking, cleaning, hostessing, calling friends. You are softer, more accessible, more porous, more tender, more playful now—and your clothes should be all of these, too. (And if you do feel pressured, your clothes can cut against this feeling, reminding you by their soft feel on your skin that this is your time.)

"This is sanctuary time for me—and you," these clothes say.

Finally, in Mood Zone 1, as your Bedroom Self, even the intimate distractions of your life have been stripped away. All tasks are done. Friends, children are gone. Alone—after bath, with book and music—or with husband or lover—you are most purely and intensely in your heart, your skin, your own body. After a day when it's been buried under so many layers, a deep sensuality that is uniquely your own finally has a chance to shine.

Let it! Dress to encourage the fantasy, passion and tenderness, the romance, rapture and delight so available to you now. Go with that self—your Best Bedroom Self.

For in that exploration, enticement—your own particular style of it—is born.

Now that you've opened your eyes, open your closet.

There. I thought so. You have plenty of clothes for your public selves. They take up most of your closet.

But for your private selves, you have practically nothing to wear.

Oh, perhaps you have a few special items of lingerie and lounge-wear, which you either treat like heirloom jewels and therefore never wear, or which you do wear—monotonously—over and over again. (Yet you wouldn't dream of wearing the same dress to the office day after day.)

I'm not counting, of course, the baggy old pants and washed-out shirts you insist on retaining, calling them your around-the-house wardrobe.

Around-the-house isn't some leftover, doesn't-matter time of your life. It's a full half of your life that very much <u>does</u> matter, because it gives rise to and nourishes your intimacies . . . because it includes the deep pleasures that make the rest of your life worth it.

Your private time is your reward time. Why shortchange yourself on that reward? In order for those hours to give you what you want, need and deserve from them, you must meet them halfway by honoring them with the right clothes.

You wouldn't dream of wearing a lace-trimmed satin slip gown to a sales conference. (Or, for that matter, a pair of old jeans.) Yet you're still wearing a tailored shirt—plus that pair of old jeans—for the few precious hours you and your husband have to switch gears from work to delight.

Sure, a mood of sensual intimacy can eventually scale the hurdle imposed by workday associations, clammy skin pinched by tight elastic and coarse, don't-touch fabric.

But why on earth should it have to?

Instead, make it easy. Make it wonderful.

The ball is in your court.

Most women are the candle-lighters, the mood-makers. Men know little or nothing about creating an atmosphere for intimacy. However, men are changing and becoming more aware—they want that intimacy. They are the grateful, and delighted, partakers of the mood women create.

You lead. He will follow. He wants to follow.

What marvelous power you've got in your hands!

Still, you have hesitations.

"Isn't building this wardrobe of beautiful intimate wear impractical?" you ask.

No. It's a myth that beautiful clothes have to be hard to care for, just as it's a myth that unattractive, "practical" clothes are necessarily comfortable.

Most of the beautiful loungewear today is made of manmade fibers. Recent technology has provided polyester fabrics—alone or in blends—with all the good looks of cotton, linen, silk and wool. The new blends are indistinguishable from natural fibers, and they are as handsome as they are practical. Polyester fits the life-style of busy, modern women. It provides all the aesthetic qualities of a natural fiber, but it resists wrinkling and is easy to care for. It can be tossed in the washer, the dryer, then over the head. Pull a pair of blue jeans from the same forty-five-minute dryer cycle from which you've just pulled the poly-charmeuse gown and the gown will look and feel wonderful on your skin, while the jeans will still be damp (requiring at least one more cycle), look tight and feel awful.

Now which of those two outfits would you rather risk spilling something on while you're fixing the eggs in the morning?

"Still," you wonder, "even if they can be washed, isn't it extravagant to have such clothes?"

Not at all. Apart from the valuable investment you are making in your self-image and self-esteem (why <u>not</u> start the day looking beautiful?), there's a sheer dollars-and-cents savings: Having a wardrobe of beautiful loungewear gives you an extra second wardrobe of glamorous evening wear at half or a third of what similar styles would cost in ready-to-wear.

You don't have to be a woman on a strict budget to appreciate this value. Nancy Kissinger was photographed in *Vogue* wearing my black halter-top floor-length gown with gold lamé belt. It cost her—and every other woman who bought it—under $100.

Finally, you ask, "But how do I know how many, and what kind of, clothes I need for this new intimate wardrobe?"

You learn the answer to this by asking your private selves some personal questions.

Putting together the intimate wardrobe that's exactly right for your unique life can be done without the waste, confusion and trial and error that are usually associated with getting a wardrobe right. All it takes is a little self-interrogation.

All the clothes I'm going to tell you about here are to be found in the intimate-apparel departments of most stores. However, they're not grouped the way I'm grouping them. More likely, they're all mixed together in different racks and on different rounders and displays.

Miss Lucy used to be your pathfinder in this department—and, oh, the wilderness of clichés she stranded you in. (To her way of thinking, harem pants should never have left ancient Persia, intimate wear just does <u>not</u> go to dinner parties . . . and <u>never</u> does it march down the aisle; and a girl can't go wrong with a good, warm belted robe.)

This time you're going to find your way yourself. You're going to leave Miss Lucy to her crossword puzzle or her letter to her sister Adele, while you select exactly the styles and fabrics that precisely (and imaginatively, and beautifully) fit nobody's intimate life but your own.

Let's start with your Private Party Self.

1. When you're giving a dinner party, you've got a built-in advantage in knowing the color scheme your visual presence will be working with. Use that advantage.

Nancy Kissinger

Do you have loungewear that is harmonious with the room you'll be entertaining in yet at the same time lets you stand out? You've gone to great trouble, no doubt, to coordinate the colors of the table setting—but how about the colors of yourself?

Factor your clothes into the overall color statement. For example, if you have a salmon-color dining room and the flowers you have chosen for the party are dogwood, creamy lilies and lilacs, you might take an accent color from the flowers and wear lilac.

2. Also at your own dinner parties, you're seated at the head of the table. All eyes are on you—from the waist up. Make that part of yourself shine. Choose a gown with a very dramatic neckline—a scoop, a one-shoulder, a V—to highlight your face. Or if you have beautiful jewels, choose a simple top of a solid color and luxe fabric (panné velvet, silk, satin, crepe de chine) that will backdrop those jewels, which, in turn, will light up your face.

3. You may be sitting at your dinner parties, but at your cocktail parties you're moving, moving, moving. You're like a whirling dervish: spinning to greet guests, introduce people, freshen drinks. Much more than at almost any other time, people see the back as well as the front of you. Make it worth seeing—and admiring. Choose for these evenings loungewear with dramatic back lines: a draped back or a low-belted back (as in a halter).

4. And since you're dashing around so much at these parties and possibly going up and down stairs, why not be comfortable—how about pants instead of a gown? A tunic-and-pant, a culotte or a jumpsuit will take you elegantly through the paces of those evenings.

As you know, one of the most important characteristics of at-home wear is comfort. It allows you ease of movement. Ease of movement means self-assurance, élan. Élan means a striking hostess and a successful party.

5. If you go to many gala balls, you can stretch your budget a bit with the beautiful, far less costly dressed-up gowns that loungewear departments feature around holiday time. Many diplomats' and congressmen's wives in Washington do just that. So do some of the savviest women, who often find themselves radiantly distinctive in a room full of this season's ready-to-wear "in"-look clones.

6. If you're young and lively and your small evening gatherings often move out to late-night clubs, you might lean to the more daring and

Barbara de Portago Grant

danceable styles—jodhpur pants with low, bandeau or wrapped tops. Or a dramatic butterfly pants and quilted kabuki jacket.

7. Are you entertaining for the holidays? Jewel-toned panné velvet caftans are lush and warm for Thanksgiving. Red silk—pajama or hostess skirt—is perfect for Christmas. A strapless satin jumpsuit topped by a three-quarter-length coat, a one-shouldered gown, a djellaba sprayed with bugle beads—all can provide drop-dead drama for New Year's Eve.

Holiday time is when the loungewear departments carry their most exciting dressed-up items. Shop now for the rest of the year as well.

8. Do you travel a lot? Loungewear's unstructuredness is a great asset. Rather than using a whole wardrobe bag for one evening gown, you can roll up two unstructured gowns, possibly in matte jersey, pack them in a space hardly bigger than a makeup case, and after a steam-out in the hotel bathroom, you're set for the evening—and the next one, as well.

9. Are you going on a cruise? This is your opportunity to wear glorious clothes that may be too delicate for city streets. Go for fabrics and styles that move with the breeze: a printed silk blouson over pants; a very floaty chiffon top over pants or a spaghetti-strap gown; a handkerchief-hem ankle-length skirt with an off-the-shoulder georgette blouse.

10. Are you taking a tropical winter vacation? Pull an oversize, over-the-head, T-shape cotton cover-up over your bathing suit to get you from your hotel room to the pool. Switch to a terry sarong over that same suit for lunch at the pool. Choose a mid-calf cotton sundress with appliqué to sightsee in town. Show off your tan with a beautiful strapless dress (in one of the luxurious polyester blends I mentioned) for dinner and nightclub.

11. Are you going on a ski vacation? For aprés ski, whether you're in Aspen, Gstaad or Stowe, a quilted reversible jacket goes double distance (you can wear one color one evening, the other the next) when teamed creatively with ready-to-wear. International socialite Barbara de Portago Grant tells me she builds a sparkly, dressy, shades-of-gray look out of gray flannel trousers, a wonderful blouse of gray georgette silk shot with silver lamé, all topped with my pale gray satin quilted jacket that's embroidered with silver thread and studded with beading. Topped off with Barbara's diamond jewelry, the look shoots silver sparks through the late-day St. Moritz snow.

12. Are you planning a wedding? Or are you going to be a member of a small wedding party? And have you waded though the racks of bridesmaid's gowns, only to find either the kinds of things your friend's great-aunt would wear to a boat christening, or those that a tenth-grader would wear to her piano recital? Loungewear offers a much more stylish—and less costly—alternative to these grimly matronly and sweetly virginal dresses that you can wear only once (which is once more than you'd like).

When Vicki Gifford was planning her wedding to Michael Kennedy (the fourth son of Robert and Ethel Kennedy), she didn't like what she saw on the bridal department racks, either. She told me she wanted something fresher, younger and more versatile for her seven young attendants. She came up to my showroom and chose a wonderfully charming lavender and white ankle-length dress that hinted at Monet maidens with parasols. A few sprays of violets and baby's breath made the dresses perfect for walking down the aisle at what turned out to be <u>the</u> social wedding of the season. And the girls got plenty of "civilian" party wear from those dresses after that.

Now, moving on to the needs of your Intimate Self . . .

You're shifting your attention from the dramatically hand-painted silks, the bugle beads and the one-shouldered gowns that fit so wonderfully with your Private Party Self to the more simple and casual pieces that are nevertheless beautiful. Some of these styles may be similar to those of the private party loungewear we just discussed (the tunic and pant, the caftan), but the fabrics you'll be looking for now are easy-care: polyester crepe de chine, polyester satin, polyester charmeuse, panné velvet, jersey, cotton and stretch terry.

This is a time when your clothes have to perform on more than just a visual level. As your Private Party Self, you were purely entertaining or being entertained. Now, as your Intimate Self, you are doing. As your Private Party Self, you wanted all-out glamour. As your Intimate Self, you're looking for practical glamour.

Here is how you find it:

13. Do you have a terrace, porch, patio or yard or windows that are visible to neighbors? If so, you want your intimate wear to be something

that can be glimpsed by strangers. You don't want to be self-conscious ("Oh, God, there's a man on the terrace—and I'm wearing this!"), but you don't want to lose one of the main delights of your Intimate Self: utter comfort of body and openness of spirit.

Wear a capped-sleeve, stretch cotton caftan with an Oriental appliqué, a fanny-wrap kimono, or an oversize gauze shirt with bright contrast pipings.

14. Are you briefly in public in the middle of your intimate time? Dashing out to pick up your child from a friend's, your husband at the train station? Intimate clothes that travel this way include the stretch terry jumpsuit, the cotton crop top over ankle-length pull-on pants, the mid-calf cotton sundress.

15. Are you the mother of a young child? You need a lot from your intimate wear! Lots of upper body room (for lifting, dressing, diapering, tickling); lots of lower body room (for chasing after and kneeling at the edge of the tub); lots of stain- and wrinkle-proof fabrics for sticky-fingered hugs and tussles.

Impossible to come up with something beautiful that meets these requirements? No! You can choose any comfortable style in polyester satin or crepe de chine (one rub of a damp rag and blow of the hairdryer, and the peanut butter and jelly are off). Or you can go with stretch terry and polyester cotton, both of which absorb water from cup-size spills and splashes without making you feel unpleasantly wet to the skin.

16. Are you pregnant? You don't have to look like a pitched pup tent or spend a fortune on a second wardrobe of mediocre clothes you may never wear again.

The beauty of loungewear now is that (1) it is, literally, beautiful and can help make you feel attractive when you're most vulnerable to not feeling that way; and (2) you can wear it well after the baby arrives.

Good for most if not all of your pregnancy are some Empire-style gowns, the float (it's narrow around the shoulders, waistless and wide), djellabas, wider caftans and mid-calf spaghetti-strapped A-line cotton sundresses.

17. Are you a dog walker, a cat owner? If you're cuddling a furry pet that sheds, you don't want to be wearing velvets or dark-colored fleecy

fabrics. Better to buy your intimate wear in smooth-feeling fabrics—polyester crepe de chine and charmeuse satins—from which pet hair can be brushed off easily.

If you're a dog walker, you're used to interrupting your intimate evening with a ten P.M. constitutional. The last thing you want to do is have to change back into public clothes now that you've finally gotten comfortable. But you cringe at the thought of trailing boudoir tricot on the street. The tunic-and-pant outfit is intimate and comfortable indoors—and makes the transition to outside.

18. Are you a single woman, unencumbered by all the things— child, yard, pregnancy, husband's train schedule—we've just been talking about? If so, you're a free spirit—and probably a fashion innovator. You love style and you live spontaneously. Your intimate time may consist of friends dropping in to watch the Grammies over take-out Chinese food . . . or a special new friend coming over for a simple gourmet dinner for two.

You may want a long slink of a dress (say, a floor-length sweater-dress), or harem pants and a bandeau top, or a camisole and pant topped by a kimono. You like to spice up your clothes, so when you look at loungewear on display in the store, factor in your own special touches. (How would that tassled scarf you brought back from Morocco look wrapping the hip of that caftan? Or your little antique vest over those harem pants?)

19. Do you work from your home, as more and more professionals are doing in these computer-communiqué eighties? Then you don't have to sit at your desk in Public Self clothes at all. You should be taking advantage of the comfort your counterparts in offices aren't allowed (avoid tight-waisted loungewear) while at the same time steering clear of styles that get in the way of your work, such as voluminous sleeves and slipping necklines. For sheer comfort—but also enough style to open the door to the mailman or a mes-senger—consider the slim-sleeved caftan, and wrapped or tunic tops over pull-on elastic-waist pants.

And, finally . . .

20. Has the world come crashing down on you? You had the worst possible day at the office . . . and the worst possible fight with your beau or husband. And the car wouldn't start, and the mechanic who finally came and

fixed it (after you had to cancel out on a play you were dying to see) charged you as much as a short Caribbean vacation.

Clothes to the rescue!

Have that rescue hanging in your closet, ready to take the place of a sauna or a masseuse.

I can't tell you what style or cut or fabric to choose. It's got to be something you see in a store and are magnetically attracted to. Like true love, you'll know it when you see it.

A friend of mine made the hard decision to leave a job she'd nearly built her life around. To fight the blues, she came home and pulled out her "rescue robe"—floor-length champagne panné velvet with yards and yards of ostrich feathers. It lifted her spirits. There are times when the most impractical clothes turn out to be the most practical of all.

Moving on to your Bedroom Self, what clothes do you need to make this time—and this self—the best it can be? Find out by questioning yourself on the rituals, feelings and yearnings of this, your most sensual time.

21. Is your prebedtime ritual some form of meditation, in which you want to strike a peaceful, contemplative mood? Choose a T-shape sleep shirt in pristine white pure cotton, possibly with lace and embroidery. It's got spiritual cleanness and modesty, and it will leave your legs free to assume the lotus position.

22. Does your prebedtime ritual consist not of quiet sitting but of movement—stretches, rhythmic flowing to music? If so, you want freedom for your body but with bedroom glamour as well. A camisole and tap pant are right for now. They're sensual and comfortable. Because this is a two-piece outfit, you get mobility from the waist as well as full upper- and lower-body freedom.

23. Are there times when neither utter quiet or spontaneous movement gives you the peace and escape you want at this time? When you yearn to escape the cares of the day so thoroughly, you almost wish you were in another civilization?

Go to that fabulous place and time. Have in your closet, ready for the trip, a marvelously Cleopatra-like pleated column gown . . . or a little ancient Greek chiton—wonderfully modern in style—with a draped top, elastic waist,

short skirt . . . or pure silk Chinese pajamas with side frog closings to take you back to the Ming dynasty.

24. We've been talking escape . . . yet sometimes you are deep in the present right before sleep. A problem or conflict must be laid to rest before you can do the same. For a sensitive talk with your husband or lover, I picture you in a long-sleeve iris blue satin gown with a lace-appliquéd yoke.

Why? Let's look at the separate elements. Blue is the calming, soothing color. The covered style doesn't allow any bareness of skin to distract from your words. The luxurious-feeling, sensual-looking fabric makes you feel pampered enough not to be on the defensive and makes him want to reach out and touch.

Finally, the lace yoke does two things: It draws his eyes to yours, where the most intense communication lies; and, because when we see lace we think of propriety and decorum (old lace doilies, tablecloths, handkerchiefs), it cautions you both to stay civilized. So the trim is used both to command attention and to temper feelings.

Now, you might not find a gown exactly like the one I've described, but the larger lesson to be learned here is to be open and attuned to the subtle emotional signals in the elements of clothes. Intimate clothes, particularly Bedroom Self clothes, have remarkable power over heart and psyche. Train yourself to find the right ones.

25. What we've just described was a very earnest, serious evening. But those aren't the only ones you have. (I hope!) What do you wear when you're in a playful, flirty, decidedly unserious mood—with him, or by yourself?

If you've got the body to wear it, a little ruffle-bottomed teddy that teases the eye just where the thigh meets the derriere has a light, flirty look. A mid-calf gown of solid-color cotton with a lace-up corset bodice and a bit of peekaboo around the bust gives you the playfulness of a nineteenth-century milkmaid. And for a more glamorous kind of unseriousness, a beautiful ostrich-feather pouf bed jacket tickles the fancy—and the nose.

26. Play is great, but not all the time. Even comediennes have their romantic moments, times to be very pretty and classically feminine, with no

puns intended and no tongues in cheek. What then? Not the clichéd high-necked Victorian. (They've been making them forever and they're always so forgettable.) Instead, choose a dropped-hip mid-calf gown with an antique-rose print on cotton lawn with lace and ribbon trim. The gown should be slightly see-through while at the same time demure in style: a marvelous paradox.

Or you can go for a high-necked, covered, solid-color cotton gown or robe with lots of lace, tucks and rosettes.

27. "Warmth at any price! (To hell with elegance!)" Have you ever felt like shouting those words? When the furnace in your country house isn't working, and rustic charm isn't warming your blood as much as it's warming your soul?

You don't have to sacrifice style. You can be elegant and warm in a beautiful gown that's brushed satin on the outside, fleece on the inside. It might be appliquéd with flowers and have a scalloped hem and sleeve.

Or go with a beautiful pair of man-tailored satin pajamas, also fleece-lined—all topped off by a fleecy, satin-appliquéd robe.

28. Another time you want to stay warm—and dry, as well—is just after the bath or shower, when you're doing your facial mask or your nails. Nothing's more luxurious than a big pure white terry robe. Go all out and have it monogrammed. Guests at the best European hotels have long delighted in the plush pampering they've gotten from the robes they found hanging on their bathroom doors. (The practice has now spread to American hotels.) Be your own guest.

29. Then there are nights when nothing might be so psychically uplifting as to imagine yourself the very picture of sophisticated glamour: the lady of the penthouse in some urban thirties or forties movie. Think of Carole Lombard and you see wonderful cream silk pajamas and a man-tailored robe or Jean Harlow in *Dinner at Eight* in a wonderful bias-cut slip gown. Your sense of authority of self can soar just by putting these on.

30. Are you an executive woman who travels frequently? Then you know how luxuriating quietly in your hotel room after one day of pressured meetings and before another is so important for the replenishment of your spirits and vitality. But what do you slip on over your sensual gown or your skin when there's a knock at the door—the room service waiter, about to bring in your late dinner or early breakfast?

There's a whole new category of robes made just for you. They're called travel robes, and they're lightweight, elegant, made of fabrics that won't wrinkle. You can throw one on over your gown—or over nothing. Choose them in cosmetic colors—soft eye-makeup hues (mauve, lavender, peach, delicate blues)—that won't drain your unmade-up face the way a sharp color might.

31. Are you going into the hospital? If so, you'll be receiving your guests in bed, so you want something lovely from the waist up—a bed jacket, not a robe, which, with the added bulk of the bed sheets, makes you feel like a mummy. Again, choose a soft cosmetic color, not black (which will bring you down) or white (which is too antiseptic).

Lifting your mood is never as important as it is now. One very elegant customer told me that whenever she knows she's going into the hospital, her maid looks over the room first and selects the Porthault linens, throw pillows and pictures that will warm up and personalize it. (And she wouldn't be caught dead without soft pink light bulbs!)

32. Are there nights when you want to give it all you've got? You want absolute passion. You want to be the embodiment of enticement.

From the charity fashion shows I've given for important men in the political, banking and sports worlds, I know what men like to see women wear to bed—and believe me, it's not a high-necked gown.

Try a midnight violet satin chemise dripping with rich black chantilly lace and sparkling with black jet beads, or a long spaghetti-strap bias gown in black satin with lace all the way up one side. Or really go for broke with a black satin teddy with lace cut high on the thigh and across the bosom. And don't forget the garter belt. (Men do love them.)

Or try the same styles in a cream or champagne color. All the classic screen goddesses of the old black-and-white movies wore white to distinguish themselves from everyone else on the screen. White became the color of sensuality back then . . . and it still is today.

All right, now you know the pieces of your intimate wardrobe. Let's make those pieces fit. Let's take a look at—and transform—you.

Chapter Three

Transformed to Entice!

T

he Clothes Doctor. That's what a buyer from Neiman-Marcus once called me. C.D., for short.

It's true. The M.D. heals the physically ailing; I heal the stylishly ailing. The M.D. does surgery on the body; I do it on the wardrobe. The M.D. enhances his or her work with a good bedside manner; I help a woman learn to enhance her own bedside manner—to throw away the fears, hesitations and misconceptions that have been holding her Intimate Self down—and to transform that self to beauty and drama.

I consider all women my patients. Here are some classic cases I would love to transform. Could one of them be a little like you?

1: T-Shirt Tomboy to Young Sophisticate

Patient's Symptoms:

The T-Shirt Tomboy is a young woman, just out of college. Sleepwear to her was whatever T-shirt she nodded out in after crash-cramming for her exam, or whatever sweater kept her warmest and didn't itch. Intimate wear? That made no sense to her as a category, since she had no intimate time in her parents' home or in her college dorm room—and where else did she ever spend after-school hours?

But it's no longer after school; now it's after work. And she no longer shares quarters—except, perhaps, with a couple of roommates. She's in her own apartment now; she's gotten more sophisticated. The fallen-into, thrown-together night look that was so cute two years ago is something she can't get away with anymore.

And why on earth should she want to, when there's a much more wonderful self to turn into, one that radiates all the youth she wants—but with a new style that befits her coming of age.

The C.D.'s Diagnosis:

Her Big Fear: That intimate wear is either too young for her (the frilly nighties of her childhood) or too old (her mother's peignoirs).

Her Big Mistake: Equating casual with sloppy, youthful with devil-may-care;

taking the lived-in look too far.

Her Big Asset: Youth! Smooth, clear skin that doesn't need much makeup to look wonderful; a good, firm body; a natural exuberance that shines through her clothes.

My Task: To turn her from awkward young girl to appealing young woman.

The transformation begins . . .

The C.D.'s Diagnosis:

She should drop all her harsh-fabric Public Self wear after five P.M.—the jeans, the sweaters, the Ts . . .

In favor of the pampered feel and comfort of a polyester satin, charmeuse or pure cotton batiste sleep shirt with lots of French lace. Or try tap pants and camisoles, teddies with fanny wraps. (Later she'll graduate to longer styles and gowns; right now she's getting used to the idea that absolute comfort and body freedom can be luxurious.)

She should also:

• Celebrate the day/night, public/private division with little changes in her environment that appeal to her youthful sense of romance: candlelight, plump floor cushions, her favorite records, pretty see-through fabric swathed over the windows. The fabulous sense of theatrical mood that she sees in her favorite music videos can be hers, enhancing her change of clothes.

• Change her hairstyle for the occasion—from day-easy to night-pretty—and experiment with combs and clips and bows.

• Change her makeup as well—to a soft and romantic look. (Experiment now, while makeup is still a magnificent novelty, not an obligation to help out Mother Nature.)

• Be sure to change her shoes. Even day sandals (like the gladiator sandals that were at one time all the vogue) say day and detract from an ethereal mood. If you're dancing at home to music, go barefoot. Or wear satin ballet slippers.

The Finished Look:

Sexy, silky, insouciant, ingenuous.

2: Trendy Wendy to Fashion Innovator

<u>Patient's Symptoms:</u>

<u>Trendy Wendy</u> is mad for style—so much so that she's almost a one-woman encyclopedia of every new look in the last three seasons. She changes from an oversize jumpsuit with kangaroo pockets and big shoulder pads for a small party . . . to the Japanese bag look for another party . . . to tailored plaid flannel on a ski trip . . . to silk harem pants on New Year's Eve—all faster than you can say <u>chameleon.</u> And her hairstyles and accessories go from punk to preppy twice as fast. Who she is, under this movable feast of gimmickry, is hard to tell. Her intimate clothes wear her instead of she wearing them.

<u>The C.D.'s Diagnosis:</u>

<u>Her Big Fear:</u> That she won't be absolutely up-to-the-minute.
<u>Her Big Mistake:</u> Letting herself be a fashion victim instead of moderating and editing fashion trends.
<u>Her Big Asset:</u> Her sharp antenna for style; her fashion bravery, and her willingness to experiment and change.
<u>My Task:</u> To change her from fashion slave to fashion original.

The transformation begins . . .

<u>The C.D.'s Prescription:</u>

<u>She should drop</u> all clothes that are cluttered, gimmicky, fussy in cut or print. No more total "buying" of a look. (A common mistake made by women like Wendy is to take a style straight off the runway or out of the pages of a magazine. When the Japanese look was in, for example, Wendy wore it all—torn hose, baggy raggy clothes, severe, pared-down makeup—without stopping to think

of what parts of it did and did not look good on her.)

In favor of a discriminating use of new fashion, an editing of the newest trends. Clothes with a simple but innovative cut that provide a clean canvas on which to paint all the variations that satisfy her need to express and to change herself: a simple, sleek-necked tunic top and pant in a variety of subtle colors (pale pastels, blacks, whites) offer an anchoring, consistent image.

She should also:

- Use jewelry and scarves to create a personal and up-to-date look.
- Keep makeup current but simple. (The more she accessorizes her body, the less she should her face.)
- Be color conscious: select one or two colors of the fashion moment instead of trying to use them all. For example, build around neutrals (wheat, cream, beige) and accent with one of the big fashion colors.
- Start collecting good, unusual accessories she can wear for a lifetime: interesting antique jewelry, special scarves, belts. She's going to phase out the fads and start to make wonderful fashion statements with real, rare things.

The Finished Look:

Assured, savvy, surprising yet tasteful, experimental yet restrained—a woman who delights in her fashionable self without letting the winds of fashion dominate her.

3: Forever Ingenue to Chic Petite

Patient's Symptoms:

The forever ingenue is often under 5 feet 3 inches and spent most of her girlhood being called cute. Now in her twenties or thirties, she's abandoned that frilly sweetness in her Public Self look—but it still dominates her intimate look. Her little Victorian nightie is like a security blanket to her: The lace and ribbons on her neck and wrists tell her husband or lover and friends, "I'm childlike."

<u>The C.D.'s Diagnosis:</u>

<u>Her Big Fear:</u>   Making the clothing transformation from little girl to responsible woman. She's secretly afraid she'll lose her safety, comfort and youthful advantage if she stops dressing like a miniature valentine.

<u>Her Big Mistake:</u>   Staying in innocent clothes far longer than is appropriate; not understanding that vulnerability and romanticism can be expressed in stylish, grown-up, appropriate ways.

<u>Her Big Asset:</u>   Her petiteness and her youthful, fresh outlook.

<u>My Task:</u>   To move her from cutesy-pie sweetness to the womanly romantic femininity she may not have known was possible.

The transformation begins . . .

<u>The C.D.'s Prescription:</u>

<u>She should drop</u> all "sweetness" clichés, especially when they're together on one gown: pussycat bows, puffed sleeves, demure prints, smocking and girlish details.

<u>In favor of</u> more unusual and sophisticated embellishments. There are many ways to say <u>romance</u> other than the overloaded, garden-party, maiden-on-the-moors look. For example, a pastel gown or chemise with French lace, possibly

touched with seed pearls—or a beautifully draped cream matte jersey Empire gown, giving the sensuality and the romance she wants without the girlish ruffles and froufrou she's outgrown.

<u>She should also:</u>

• Change her jewelry from tiny little chain and tiny little earrings to something more important, without overpowering her. Wear one important piece instead of two unimportant ones.

• Wear bare, eveninglike slippers that have some heel to them, to glamorize and heighten the Private Party Self look or the intimate at-home look.

• Remember that many of the most glamorous movie stars—Gloria Swanson, Carole Lombard, Joan Crawford, Marilyn Monroe—were short—and look at the fabulously glamorous gowns <u>they</u> wore! It's not that you can't wear any of the more dramatic proportions when you're petite; you just have to scale them down to you, just as Joan Collins does today.

The Finished Look:

Romantic in an uncluttered, clean, womanly way, reinforcing soft, feminine knowingness instead of coy, forced girlish innocence.

4: Pajama Preppy to Classicist

Patient's Symptoms

The Pajama Preppy spent all her youth looking "appropriately" tailored, sporty, free of frills. That was fine on the boarding-school volleyball court and in the college dorm or classroom, but now her classic flannel pajama-and-robe set is distressingly dull, and her tailored silk shirt-and-pant (or long skirt) at her own dinner parties is just a rerun of the same style she goes to work in (with her running shoes, stock tie and briefcase).

The C.D.'s Diagnosis:

Her Big Fear: Calling undue attention to herself during her intimate hours. Frilly, to her, equals silly. And isn't anything more dramatic kind of . . . well, theatrical and cheap?

Her Big Mistake: Staying buttoned and belted, actually and emotionally; being unable to switch her moods from day to night.

Her Big Asset: Her refinement, her decorum, her love of classics.

My Task: To switch her from dull understatement to elegant refinement.

The transformation begins . . .

The C.D.'s Prescription:

She should drop most intimate wear that closely mimics her Public Self clothes: man-tailored pajamas, wool flannel robes, long plaid wool fireside skirts.

In favor of easier, softer interpretations of classic styles in more glamorous fabrics, for example, a white-on-white satin jacquard overblouse with matching bias pants; or a hammered satin tunic that sashes at the hip over wide-legged pants with trapunto (quilted) trim. She then acquires the wonderful look of simple, elegant, classic style, such as Katharine Hepburn was known for.

<u>She should also:</u>

• Take off her watch; change from her ultraconservative daytime jewelry to one long, beautiful drape of large pearls.

• Change right away, as soon as she enters her Private Self zone, from her daytime underwear to a lacy bra (or no bra), tap pants and camisole, teddy, all in the softest silk . . . and all to make her feel more sensual, less tailored from the skin out.

The Finished Look:

Elegant, classic, modern and glamorous.

5: Fredericka of Hollywood to Subtle Sensualist

Patient's Symptoms

<u>Fredericka of Hollywood</u> doesn't have a problem with hiding an Intimate Self behind too much sweetness or restraint. No, she has the opposite problem: In an attempt to look glamorous, she looks a bit . . . well, obvious. It's not that she wants to limit herself to plunge-neck burgundy tricot and gowns that are slit like the Grand Canyon; it's just that she doesn't really know what else there is to choose from.

The C.D.'s Diagnosis:

<u>Her Big Fear:</u>   That her own innate, natural sensuality somehow isn't enough without embellishment.

<u>Her Big Mistake:</u>   Thinking that overobvious nighttime dressing is the only way to look enticingly sensuous.

<u>Her Big Asset:</u>   A frank sensuality and pride in her body that she isn't afraid to show.

<u>My Task:</u>   To class up her act!

The transformation begins . . .

She should drop the see-through baby-dolls with the maribou trim; anything mesh or net; thigh-high slits; painted-on-tight pajamas; intimate wear that shows everything at once (you're sexier when something's hidden).

In favor of a look that plays up just one part of her body (her best part) and keeps the rest beautifully clothed. For example, if she has beautiful cleavage, she might wear a V-neck halter, or if she has a beautiful back, a wonderful low-cut back edged in lace. If her legs are her best asset, she might wear a short chemise trimmed in chantilly lace.

She should also:

• Wear less and lighter makeup and perfume.
• Simplify the hair and avoid too much teasing.
• Take off those fake gold-lamé high-heeled backless slippers for a more elegant evening shoe.
• Wear dramatic jewelry—Greek gold chokers, big drop earrings—sparingly, not all at the same time. Let them be a marvelous statement, a finishing touch.

The Finished Look:

Classy sensuality that's sure enough of itself not to have to shout.

6: Clubwoman to Glorious Hostess

Patient's Symptoms

The Clubwoman is a social, civic- and charity-minded wife and mother in her late thirties through sixties. She has taste; she has influence. She is active and respected in her circle and in her city. But that strong sense of authority that is so much her stamp in her community work often fades to an unnecessarily low gloss when she entertains in her own home.

For instead of wearing something special that sets her off as the hostess, she retreats to the same kind of cocktail dresses she wears out to public events and to other people's parties. It's time to put a little of the dash and class she invests in her volunteer work into her Private Party Self.

<u>The C.D.'s Diagnosis:</u>

<u>Her Big Fear:</u> That if she dresses dramatically at her own party, she'll look different from her guests.

<u>Her Big Mistake:</u> Not understanding how the festive cue a hostess's dress sends can add to her guests' relaxation, her party's spirit and glow. (So in a very real sense, she can do a private service to her guests in much the same way she is used to doing public service to her charity work.)

<u>Her Big Asset:</u> Her beautiful home, marvelous parties, social skills and authority—all begging to be completed by a sparkling hostess image.

<u>My Task:</u> To spark up her conservative party look with a shot of grand style and good taste.

The transformation begins . . .

<u>The C.D.'s Prescription:</u>

<u>She should drop</u> the cocktail suits, structured dresses, "little black dress" that is so right for her Public Evening Self.

<u>In favor of</u> a sweeping, dramatic look: frankly soft, luxurious materials (silk, chiffon, crepe de chine, hammered satin, panné velvet) in dramatic long styles: sumptuous caftans with wonderful appliqué or embroidery; dressy, full-skirted satin culottes; bugle-beaded tunic and pants.

<u>She should also:</u>

• Let go of the safe little pearls at her neck and on her ears. Instead, show off her beautiful traditional jewels. Or try bolder strokes with the jewelry-as-art look: flat, hammered discs hanging from a silk cord; twisted gold and stone chokers; chunky wooden ethnic beads.

<u>The Finished Look:</u>

International-hostess confidence and drama with utter refinement and taste.

7: Mom-in-a-Robe to Mother-in-Mode

Mom-in-a-Robe is a full-time homemaker or a working mom. She lives for her family, which is wonderful. But she looks so lived-in around the house that no one's spirits get the true boost they deserve from the warmth she has to offer.

Love may mean you never have to say I'm sorry, but that shouldn't be because your clothes have already said it. And a worn robe, nondescript housedress and old scuffs are sorry indeed!

The C.D.'s Diagnosis:

Her Big Fear: That pretty clothes are impractical.

Her Big Mistake: Not understanding that her family would feel all the more nurtured by her if she nurtured her own intimate look.

Her Big Asset: A warm heart, an essential womanliness that absolutely radiates through whatever she wears.

My Task: To take the dowdiness out of her maternal role and to make her as stylish as she is soothing by introducing her to at-home options.

The transformation begins . . .

The C.D.'s Prescription:

She should drop knee-length button-up housedresses, the sloppy belted cotton chenille robe, the twenty-four-hour jogging suit and all (and I mean all) slippers that look like small furry animals.

In favor of wonderful caftans in happy colors (blue, jade, yellow, pink) in solids or prints, with front zippers and easy openings; cotton hip-length tunics and pants, to break out of the gown-and-robe habit. And when she does wear a robe, a beautiful sherbet-colored fleece (rainbow and sherbet colors enhance the face and soften the process of aging), with a satin-flower appliqué. A pretty satin slipper, with style.

<u>She should also:</u>

- Always "finish" her hair, even if she's just come out of the shower. A twist at the nape of the neck and the addition of a decorative hair comb can give wet, just-washed hair a polished look.
- Take that extra few minutes to pamper herself with fresh makeup, perfume or cologne.

<u>The Finished Look:</u>

A warm, nurturing, loving woman whose sparkling style has a positive, healing effect on her family.

8: Rococo Rose to Decorous Doyenne

<u>Patient's Symptoms</u>

Rococo Rose wears it all: feathers, jewels, lace and beads. There isn't a boa feather she hasn't constricted herself in, a bugle bead she's left buried, a stone— whether real or fake—left unturned. The trouble is, it's hard to see her through all the layers of froufrou. She needs to do herself justice by removing the clutter in her intimate style while at the same time not turning down the glamour voltage in that style.

<u>The C.D.'s Diagnosis:</u>

<u>Her Big Fear:</u>   That simple is staid, mousy; that less isn't more but, rather, a bore.

<u>Her Big Mistake:</u>   Assuming that drama and impact are made from a frothed-up look from head to toe. (In fact, they're really made by the artful balance between something and nothing, a clean look skillfully decorated with the right, rare, perfectly placed ornament and detail.)

<u>Her Big Asset:</u>   Her flair, her theatricality, her embracing of ornament that other women shy from.

<u>My Task:</u>   To sleeken and simplify her look without discouraging her love of embellishment.

The transformation begins . . .

<u>The C.D.'s Prescription:</u>

<u>She should drop</u> any gowns and ensembles that are excessively ornamental or that feature more than one decoration (feathers, appliqué, beading); any gowns or ensembles that are both top-detailed (with jewels and appliqué, say) and bottom-detailed (front-slitted, say, and fringed); excessively stagey styles and trims.

<u>In favor of</u> styles that focus the drama on just one part of the body. A neckline-focusing style would be a panné velvet gown with an embroidered gold and pearl-studded neckpiece, which gives her a sleeker look with embellishment. A style that focuses on the hem might be a georgette blouse and silk taffeta skirt with a hemline in points that are embroidered and beaded. And a style that brings drama to the hip could be a hammered satin tunic over pants with jeweling and draping on the hip.

<u>She should also:</u>

• Wear simple but still important jewelry—used as a finishing touch instead of pouring it on in layers.

<u>The Finished Look:</u>

Fashion bravado that whispers rather than trumpets.

Chapter Four

Heavenly Bodies

Acouple of years ago I was having tea in the garden with my friend Jane at the famous Swiss clinic La Prairie. Across from us sat a European socialite who has lined up titled suitors and husbands throughout her life as if they were customers at a diamond-district fire sale.

From the smitten look on the face of the Bolivian tin heir seated across from her, that line was going strong.

"I saw her this morning, lying on the table waiting for her masseuse," Jane whispered. "She's got crepey arms, a thick waist and a sagging fanny. What do all those men see in her—her <u>mind</u>?"

"It's probably what they <u>don't</u> see," I opined.

"I'm not talking about the haven't-we-met-somewhere stage when they bump into each other in the aisle of the Concorde," Jane said. She was quick to correct what she supposed was my misinterpretation. "You can disguise anything at the very beginning. I'm talking about once she actually gets them in her bedroom."

"So," I said, "am I."

Jane's astonishment was typical of most women who, however sophisticated they may be, don't understand that you can disguise figure problems even in the most figure-revealing clothes . . . and that you can turn the eye <u>away</u> from imperfect parts of the body and to your best features in dozens of ways.

I discovered an even hundred, when prompted by that afternoon with Jane, I began to count the ways. I've used those ways—those tips—over the years in my designs. And I've used them in my fitting-room advice to many individual customers.

Now it's time to actually write them down and illustrate them for all of you.

If You're	Don't Wear
Quite short and fairly slim	A gown or pajama that's mid-calf or knee-length; you'll look cut in half. The mid-calf length tends to make you look shorter.
Unusually tall and thin	An Empire-style nightgown (which will only accentuate your length) or a one-shoulder gown (which draws the eye up your body vertically).
Voluptuous (size 12 or 14)	The djellaba—it's great volume tends to add inches.
Full-figured (size 16 +)	The slim caftan—it will overemphasize the fullness of your figure.

Head-to-Heel Hints . . .

nd Playing Down Your Flaws

Instead: Do Wear . . .

Something either very long and close to the body—a figure-hugging, clear-to-the-floor gown

or something very short—a short teddy and a fanny wrap—to give the illusion of lengthening your legs.

One of those marvelously chic new lengths, for example, a mid-calf sleep gown (not every woman can wear this dramatic proportion),

a caftan shape with a sash at the hip or a voluminous djellaba (your reediness looks wonderful swathed in all that volume).

The caftan, with its straight line and set-in sleeves, dolman sleeves or kimono sleeves will be perfect. Try a variety of necklines and choose the one that will flatter you most. Also, the loose top over long culottes is a flattering look for you.

Also, a slim tunic over pants that covers your thighs and derriere.

Loose, flowing caftans or a djellaba with a pretty color or a flattering neckline, for the attractive roominess you need.

If You're	Don't Wear
Very curvy and hourglass-figured	A waistless sleep chemise that adheres closely to your bust and hips but doesn't reveal your waist; it will overemphasize the two "ends" of your hourglass while ignoring totally the nipped waist that makes your shape so wonderful.
Short-necked	A high-necked gown—it'll make your neck look even shorter (if not nonexistent).
Long- but thin-necked, with prominent collarbones	Gowns with low-cut necklines or strapless.

Instead: Do Wear . . .

A hostess gown of matte jersey, satin or other body-clinging sensuous material with a sashed or tied waist, so you can pull yourself all the way in at the middle and show off your splendid curves to the tasteful hilt, like the hourglass dress I designed specifically for this figure.

A deep V-neck gown,

a halter-neck deep V wrap

or a strapless neckline.

These will lengthen your neck by drawing the eye down to the apex of your bosom.

Sleep gowns and robes with collars that are bowed, scalloped or ruffled. You want softness around the neck that will emphasize your face, and they do just that.

Or for a drop dead glamorous hostess look, one of my favorite styles is a boat-neck gown with a low draped cowl displaying a beautiful, sensuous back.

If You're	Don't Wear
Large-busted	A high-neck gown
	or a tight-bodiced gown.
Small-busted	A strapless gown (you need a little more to hold it up)
	or any sleep or hostess gown with quilted cups.
A prosthesis wearer	Anything too fitted
	or gowns that show too much cleavage.

Instead: Do Wear . . .

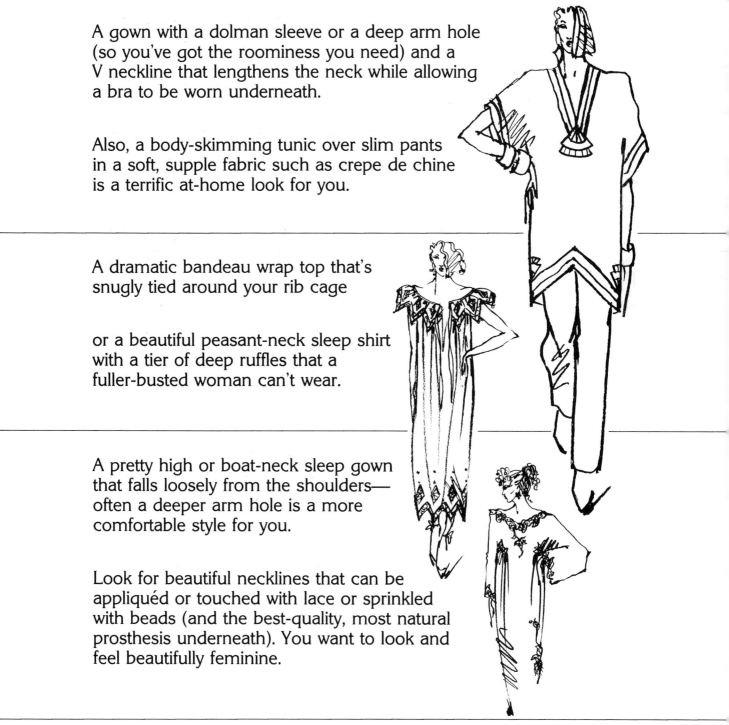

A gown with a dolman sleeve or a deep arm hole
(so you've got the roominess you need) and a
V neckline that lengthens the neck while allowing
a bra to be worn underneath.

Also, a body-skimming tunic over slim pants
in a soft, supple fabric such as crepe de chine
is a terrific at-home look for you.

A dramatic bandeau wrap top that's
snugly tied around your rib cage

or a beautiful peasant-neck sleep shirt
with a tier of deep ruffles that a
fuller-busted woman can't wear.

A pretty high or boat-neck sleep gown
that falls loosely from the shoulders—
often a deeper arm hole is a more
comfortable style for you.

Look for beautiful necklines that can be
appliquéd or touched with lace or sprinkled
with beads (and the best-quality, most natural
prosthesis underneath). You want to look and
feel beautifully feminine.

If You're	Don't Wear
Short-waisted	Any gown or robe that has a wide waistband or wide belt, or any style that makes an abrupt color change at the waist.
Long-waisted	Any gown or robe with a high armhole (it'll just make your torso look longer) or any dropped-waist or hip-sashed gown.
Small-waisted	Anything that hides that wonderful asset. (Loose pajamas, caftans and waistless gowns are for women less fortunate than you!)

Instead: Do Wear . . .

A wonderful unwaisted style, like a bra-cup chemise

or a straight-lined Empire-style sleep gown (particularly good to give the illusion of height on a short woman).

A strapless, straight-line hostess sarong gown that ties at the bust is also marvelous for you, particularly if you're average-busted.

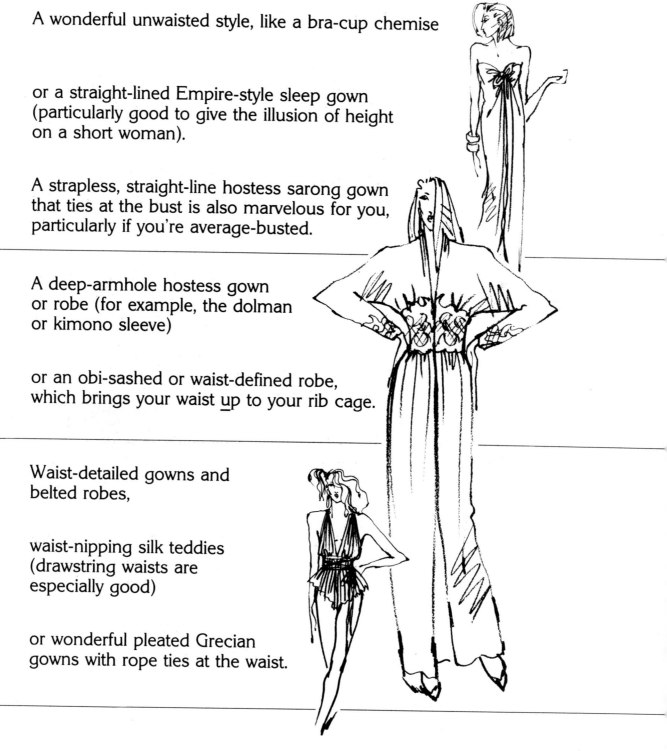

A deep-armhole hostess gown or robe (for example, the dolman or kimono sleeve)

or an obi-sashed or waist-defined robe, which brings your waist _up_ to your rib cage.

Waist-detailed gowns and belted robes,

waist-nipping silk teddies (drawstring waists are especially good)

or wonderful pleated Grecian gowns with rope ties at the waist.

If You're	Don't Wear
Thick-waisted	Anything that emphasizes or draws in at the waist.
Pear-shaped	Bias-cut clinging sleep gowns or hip-sashed tunics over pants.
Medium-tall and hippy	A crop top and pants or anything that wraps or ties at the hip.

Instead: Do Wear . . .

A loose-skimming gown that draws attention to the neckline or yoke,

an Empire

or dropped-hip style that skims the waist.

A gown that floats out over the hips and thighs, with a beautiful neckline to bring attention to the face and neck.

A hostess style that I made popular that I call the float—a style which is a pyramid shape—small at the top and flowing at the hem.

A mid-calf tunic over pants, Indian style. It falls straight, and you've got the height to wear this wonderful style in cotton gauze or hammered satin.

Or a T-shape sleep gown with an Empire cut and shirring over the hip.

For an elegant hostess look, try a strapless Empire-style in a not-too-clingy fabric.

If Your	Don't Wear
Fanny sags	Any style made of an especially soft, clingy material, like jersey.
Fanny protrudes	Any gown or pajama pant that cups in tightly over your bottom or that has a tightly defined waist.
Thighs show cellulite	Anything cut high on the sides (a teddy, for example) or a tight bias-cut gown.
Thighs and legs are shapely	Anything that will cover them up! And don't wear gowns that just cover the knee; you're hiding the best curves in your leg.
Legs are shapeless, bony or chunky	Teddies, sleep shirts or chemises. And don't wear mid-calf gowns, which cut the legs at an unattractive point.

Instead: Do Wear . . .

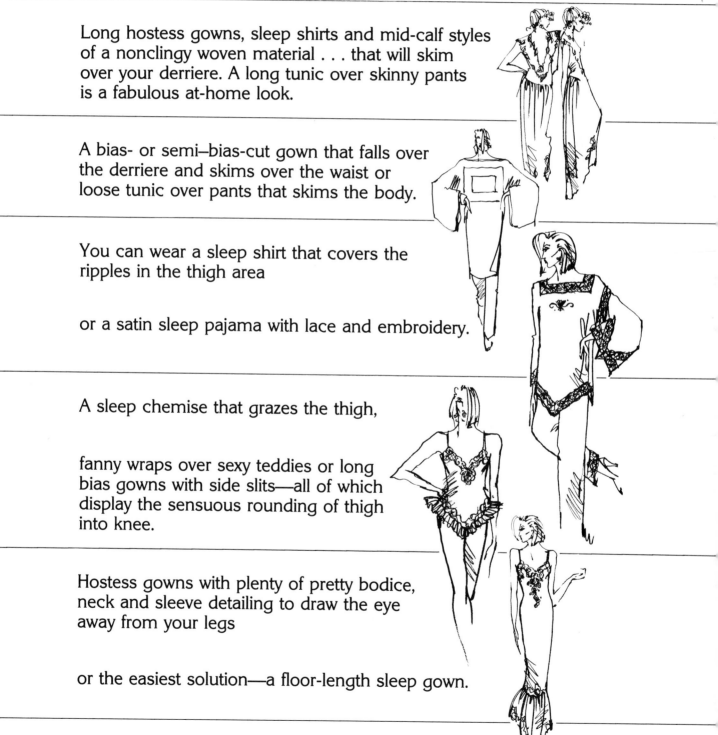

Long hostess gowns, sleep shirts and mid-calf styles of a nonclingy woven material . . . that will skim over your derriere. A long tunic over skinny pants is a fabulous at-home look.

A bias- or semi–bias-cut gown that falls over the derriere and skims over the waist or loose tunic over pants that skims the body.

You can wear a sleep shirt that covers the ripples in the thigh area

or a satin sleep pajama with lace and embroidery.

A sleep chemise that grazes the thigh,

fanny wraps over sexy teddies or long bias gowns with side slits—all of which display the sensuous rounding of thigh into knee.

Hostess gowns with plenty of pretty bodice, neck and sleeve detailing to draw the eye away from your legs

or the easiest solution—a floor-length sleep gown.

Chapter Five

Shed the Day—
Embrace the Night

Clothes, as we've seen, play a very big part in changing you from your Public to your Intimate Self. But clothes aren't all of it. Picture yourself coming home tired, feeling put-upon and keyed up from a long day. There's mail to open, a meal to prepare, the reality of a not-entirely-perfect house.

You face up to all these things. And then, right away, you pull off your tight suit and slip into a wonderful tunic and pants or an easy caftan. The clothes make you feel great. But how far is it going to take you in changing the mood of the day? About halfway: halfway toward slowing the pace of your breathing, loosening your tensed shoulders, straightening your spine . . . halfway toward diminishing your anxieties . . . halfway toward feeling romantic.

But halfway isn't enough. Glamour is magic, and with magic, there's no in between.

It just doesn't make sense to waste a wonderful gown when the body underneath hasn't been prepared to enjoy that gown to its fullest.

You deserve more. You deserve magic.

You deserve to come home and enter an entirely different world from the one you've lived in all day.

And to get what you deserve, you need a ritual, a rite of passage from Public to Intimate Self; a soothing bridge from practicality to romance; a luxurious cleansing of the body and the spirit. With that rite of passage, you shed one set of clothes—your public daywear—and don another—your intimate attire.

Many women I know perform this ritual instinctively, and each woman has her own unique plan. For example:

• When she comes home at dusk, New York socialite Anne Slater takes off the blue-lensed glasses she always wears on the street (blue is the soothing color), bathes in a room lighted all in pink (the romance color), then puts on her evening face sitting at a sumptuous mirrored dressing table that once belonged to Brenda Frazier, the most glamorous debutante of the thirties.

That's how she turns into her Intimate Self.

• Another woman I know, whom I shall simply call The Diplomat's Wife, leaves her Chanel-suited propriety behind her at 5 P.M. Safe within the residential wing of the Ambassador's Residence in the foreign capital—down the hall from the

public rooms in which, just one hour earlier, she'd poured tea for a visiting dignitary—she lies on satin sheets in a beautiful draped four-poster bed whose canopy is discreetly (but thoroughly) lined with a dazzling mirror.

That's how <u>she</u> turns into <u>her</u> Intimate Self.

Although these women have social cachet, great style and wealth, it doesn't really take any of these things to fashion a mood-shifting ritual just as marvelous—just as healing, soothing and glamorizing—as theirs. It doesn't even take what may be the busy woman's hardest-won commodity: time. In fact, it takes only thirty minutes by the clock.

It all starts with the understanding that . . .

Your Bath Is Your Sanctuary

If you are going to wash away the cares of the day at five or six P.M., you must do so literally. Not only is the skin healed when it's immersed in water; the entire self is refreshed, relaxed—reborn—in the bath.

At the end of the day, like a stage manager deftly changing a Broadway show set between scenes, you must change the entire mood of your bathroom from one that gets you briskly off and out into the day world to one that pampers you into ultimate relaxation and seduces you into the mysteries of evening.

You want a bathroom that's a glorious lair—the kind of indulgent retreat in which Mary, Queen of Scots, bathed in wine and France's Madame Tallien in crushed raspberries and strawberries.

The kind of place where you can feel that the environment is utterly tuned to your comfort—as Jackie Onassis must feel when she walks upon her specially heated marble bathroom floor.

You want a bathroom sumptuous enough to give a party in. (Lady Mendell, one of the most famous decorators and international personalities of the thirties, started it all by having bathroom soirées at which the guests reclined on chintz chaises. All her international friends were dying to be invited.)

But the party you're giving at day's end is a lavish one for one honored guest—you.

These are some of the supplies you might need for your ritual:

- A beautiful bath tray that fits over your bathtub. It could be done in steel or Plexiglas or washed gold finish.
- Your favorite collection of fragrant soaps or bath oils. Why not try some of the aromatic apothecary soaps? Stores such as Caswell-Massey or Crabtree and Evelyn specialize in unusual items you don't find at ordinary drugstores. You might try matching your bath soap and bath oil fragrances.
- Four scented candles—to match or contrast the soaps and oils.
- For your libations, either:

a lovely china cup and saucer, and a pot of steaming tea

—or—

a beautiful long-stemmed crystal wineglass and a chilled bottle of your favorite wine.

- Pink lightbulbs.
- Your favorite mood-inspiring music, whether it's from built-in speakers or a small portable tape-cassette player.
- A loofah mitt and an oversize natural sponge. Tropical-island people learned the secrets of keeping their skin soft and smooth with the loofah.
- Items for your facial mask and for the removal of your makeup.
- A good pumice stone or pumice soap.
- A pretty hair ribbon or marvelous terry turban to keep your hair dry.
- A tiny, elegant hand-mirror.
- A small, attractive timer.
- A pretty little wood or steel basket, the handle of which will fit over the tub spout (or if you really want to treat yourself, a little silver basket from Tiffany's), that you can fill with combinations of fresh herbs: chamomile and elder for their soothing, healing effect; lavender, jasmine, mint for fragrance; rose petals for luxury.
- A floatable bath pillow.
- A beautiful lacquered bowl in which to float one exotic flower—a gorgeous lotus or gardenia.

You might try for added luxury:

- Heated towel racks.
- A portable whirlpool attachment (or if you happen to be remodeling your bathroom, this is the time to build one in).
- A light-dimmer system.

Finally, you'll need:

- A chaise lounge, either in the bathroom itself or right outside, in your bedroom or dressing area. It might be nice to have a lush terry throw on it for after the bath. You may want to try what the Japanese use—a futon, a padded mattress that goes on the floor. Or if you're a real health enthusiast, a slant board to get the circulation moving.
- And don't forget how much mirrors can heighten the bath.
- If you want a more therapeutic bath, try some soothing sea salts.
- Have on hand a wonderful, big, fluffy terry robe, some natural-bristle nail brushes, some dusting powders in your favorite fragrances, perhaps matching your soaps and bath oils, and some body lotions, spray body oils and the latest in keeping your skin fresh—mineral water sprays.

Your thirty-minute mood-shifting ritual is your free time. No one's allowed to intrude. If necessary, tell them, "Hold your tongues, hold your news, hold the mail, hold your breath if you have to, and start counting to eighteen hundred slowly."

Okay, now that we've got all the preliminaries taken care of, let's get to the ritual itself.

Phase I: Feed Your Senses (All Six of Them)— 15 Minutes

With the pink lights very low and the bath-side candles lit, you immerse yourself in the warm water into which you have poured scented oils or bath salts . . . and you open all your senses to the experience.

Let your sense of <u>sight</u> be delighted by the soft pink hue of the room, the dappling pattern the flickering candlelight makes on the water, the way the light and shadow play so beautifully on all the objects and textures.

Breathe deeply of the aromatic herbs that are sending their healing fragrance into the air as the bathwater trickles through them. Let your sense of <u>smell</u> be delighted by those herbs, as in ancient times, when these aromatics were used to relax, stimulate and rejuvenate.

<u>Hear</u> the music on the cassette. Any kind of classical music—from full symphony to string quartet—is marvelous. So is Oriental music, Indian sitar music, Gershwin, Billie Holiday, Pavarotti, Irving Berlin. Or best of all are natural sound effects: gentle rain, wind through a wheat field. My personal favorite is the sound of the ocean.

<u>Taste</u> the tea, the wine or the sherry. Savor it slowly. A Manhattan hostess and author tells me, "I always sip a thimbleful of sherry during my six o'clock bath. It soothes you without tiring you."

<u>Feel</u> the warmth of the oil-softened water on every inch of your skin. Stretch out on your pillow and elongate your body; then breathe deeply and feel, too, your breath replenishing and calming you. The bath touches the central nervous system. Proper breathing is life, according to top model and author Carmen, who has been staying beautiful for over forty years. "My beauty ritual is breathing. I like it because I can control it. I don't need a masseur or a machine. It's just between me and my bath." (Check to see that you're doing deep-abdominal breathing correctly. Imagine your lungs as balloons. The bottom of the balloon, when blown into, expands first. Put one hand just below your diaphragm, the other hand on your chest. Take a deep breath. If the hand on your diaphragm raises before the hand on your chest, you're breathing correctly.)

Now that you've concentrated on each sense individually, and now that you're breathing deeply, integrate the senses. Experience the whole: all sensations together. And from this calming yet elevated state, let your sixth sense emerge.

Close your eyes now and heal them from the day's heavy dose of artificial light by placing over each a witch-hazel-dipped cotton square (Diana Vreeland does this lying flat on her marble bathroom floor) or the thinnest circle of cucumber. Many models prefer this natural approach. Either way, you'll tone the eye membranes and soothe tired eyes.

      With your eyes closed, let your sixth sense wander. Let the sum of pampering sensations that are being received by your five senses propel you to another world. How about Cleopatra's bath, with her fragrant oils and her plumed fans? Or running through a tropical rain forest, all lush and green, with gentle drops of rain caressing your shoulders? Or imagine yourself floating in midair, gliding with the gentle spring breeze. And, most important, take time to visualize your evening. How do you want to be perceived by people? What kind of rapport do you want to create? What kind of image do you want to project? Elegant? Sensual? You can create your mystique. How we perceive ourselves is what is seen by others. What you can visualize you can obtain.

Phase II: Stimulation—10 Minutes

      Time to get all the cells of your body moving again.

      Apply your facial mask, if you have one, to tone your skin and tighten your pores.

      Take the pumice stone or pumice soap and use it on elbows and heels to slough off the dry skin, to soften and beautify. When you're wearing Intimate Self clothes, these parts of your body show more, so you particularly want them looking lovely and feeling great. This is also the time to take out your beautiful nail brushes and do your nails.

      Do ten complete, slow head rolls clockwise, then ten counter-clockwise.

      Give your feet a massage. The science of reflexology, which is given credibility in Eastern philosophy and in Western medicine, tells us that there's a point on the foot that corresponds, through the nervous system, with every organ in the body. So when you're massaging your feet, you're promoting stimulation and well-being throughout your body.

      Try cradling your foot in hand. Bearing down gently with your thumb on the sole of the foot, make little circles from the area right in front of the heel to right in front of the ball of the foot. Then press your thumb straight up, from heel to toes, about five times, all across the sole from left to right.

Next, make little circles on the ball of the foot, from under the big toe to under the little toe. Now gently twist each toe.

Finally, working on the front of the foot, run your middle three fingers down between the bones of the foot from toe to ankle. Repeat five times. Top it all off by massaging the heel in gentle circles.

Now you're ready for . . .

Phase III: The Recline—5 Minutes

Step out of the tub. While your skin is still moist, apply your body moisturizer to allow the body to absorb the moisture it has lost through the day. Dust yourself with powder. Wrap yourself in your plush terry robe. Go to the chaise lounge; elevate your feet to clear your head and rush the blood to your heart. This will give you energy—and passion—for the evening. If you like, brush your hair vigorously with a natural-bristle hairbrush (with a wonderful handle of carved ivory, tortoiseshell or silver) from scalp to tips in this same upside-down position. Touch your pulse points with your favorite fragrance. The natural warmth of your body will keep your fragrance alive throughout the evening. But be sure to choose fragrances that are not too strong or too heavy (some women's biggest mistake). I don't think that the cologne should precede the woman. And always apply a touch of fragrance before you're going to bed.

After five minutes, get up. You'll be amazed at the spring in your step. Do your face; do your hair; get dressed in something absolutely fabulous.

And now, with your Intimate Self in full flower, get on with a perfectly enticing evening.

Chapter Six

The Power of Color

Your bath ritual helped move you toward a mood of enticement. Your Intimate Self clothes brought you the rest of the way.

Now you have to sustain that marvelous mood—to nourish and encourage it so that it extends throughout the whole evening.

And that you do with your surroundings.

You must set your Intimate Self on the right stage. You must ensconce yourself in an atmosphere that enhances and highlights the mood you've so skillfully and stylishly brought out in yourself, be it glamour, romance or relaxation. You want to use that atmosphere, too, to invite others into that mood—to envelop them in it, to captivate them with it.

How do you do all this?

You start with color.

Color is power. It's not just an incidental element in our lives—not a mere decorative touch. Rather, color touches our feelings, our spirit, sometimes even our bodies, deeply and profoundly.

Color is serious business (though we can have great, grand fun with it, too—and we will in a minute). It's a force—an energy—a tool. It is one of the most powerful mood makers of all.

I learned this when I was on a yacht party in Australia a number of years ago. The yacht was furnished with exquisite antiques. The food was marvelous and the champagne, first-rate.

Still, as the yacht entered Sydney Harbor at sunset, everyone gasped. With the brilliant orange meeting the dark blue water and throwing a prismic rainbow out on the horizon like an emperor's cloak . . . with the glorious white walls of the new Opera House rising above that water like swans' wings . . . it seemed as if the colors of that exact place and moment were sending out a symphonic greeting.

"What impact color has," I marveled to another guest.

"I know," he agreed. "At the hospital where I'm chief surgeon, we've just painted all the recovery rooms green. New medical research has shown that wounds actually heal faster in green rooms."

Ever since that day my exploration of color began in earnest. With the help and guidance of New York decorator John Robert Moore II, whose noted for his unexpected combinations of color, I redecorated my living room in colors that shimmered and blazed with a special energy: lacquered watermelon walls . . . sky-blue taffeta draperies with pale lime silk undercurtains . . . and a blue-and-white Indo-Chinese rug. Then I filled the room with English and French antiques.

The effect of the watermelon and blue was electric on everyone who entered the room. I had some of my best parties there. The conversation was charged yet convivial, never antagonistic. People talked to each other intensely, at a high-energy pitch. Yet they were also wonderfully relaxed. It seemed like a marvelous best of both worlds.

"That," explained a friend well versed in Eastern philosophy, "is because orange has always been considered the color that brings out the energy of the intellect, and blue, the color of calmness, of spiritual healing. Since both colors are present in equal force in your room, you are both stimulating your guests' minds and relaxing their emotions. No wonder you have such great parties there!"

Fascinated by my friend's assessment, I decided to go one step further to see what science had to say about it. I found that a man by the name of Henner Ertel, director of a national psychology institute in Munich, Germany, had recently tested schoolchildren over a three-year period and found that when the classrooms they were in were painted orange, their social behavior improved. The children cheered up and felt less hostile and irritable.*

As for blue, I found that a European doctor by the name of Ponza had tested the color in a mental hospital in 1875 and found: "A violent case who had to be kept in a strait jacket was shut in the room with the blue window; less than an hour afterwards, he had become calmer."† (And it wouldn't be a bad idea for me to have a pair of blue-lensed glasses like my friend Ann Slater's when I fly to Europe for fashion shows . . . and my entire collection is delayed, misplaced and picked over by foreign customs agents for three hours!)

And:

• Do you know how Claire Boothe Luce is rumored to have gotten Henry Luce to break up his marriage for her? She dressed herself in pure white and ensconced herself in a white-on-white hotel suite (with lots of white flowers, of

* Faber Birren, *Color and Human Response* (New York: Van Nostrand Reinhold, 1978), p. 51.
† Ibid, p. 44.

course) and invited him up. There she cried into a white linen hankie about her anguish at the lack of respectability of their alliance. All that spiritual purity made poor Henry's knees buckle, and he gave in (without even knowing that was what he was doing!).

• And do you know why the customers of Elizabeth Arden always feel pampered to the hilt? They're beautified under pink lights, in pink-walled rooms, wearing pink robes and swathed in pink towels. (For a similar reason—with a decidedly different clientele—a lot of police stations are now featuring pink-walled interrogation rooms. I guess the officers would rather pamper than browbeat their suspects into revealing their crimes. So much more civilized that way!)

• And did you know that yellow has always been considered the color of wisdom? Indian holy men wear saffron yellow robes. And I don't for a minute think it's a coincidence that Wallis Simpson, one of the few women who have made yellow their trademark color, had the smarts to lure the future king of England, Edward VIII, off the throne and to become the Duchess of Windsor.

• And speaking of Wallis and Edward, there was Lady Diana Cooper, a stylish figure of the early twentieth century, who was courted by the Duke, too, but, despite her title, lost him to Wallis. Poor Lady Diana, she lost a party guest, too—to the color of passion: red. Seems she had a little dinner party one evening in her infamous flaming red dining room, and right between courses, one of her guests stood and shot another guest dead. (At least the bloodstains were less conspicuous that way.)

So, as we've seen, green (as my surgeon friend told me in Sidney) heals and gives life; yellow projects wisdom; white radiates purity. And red impassions; orange energizes the intellect and cheers the spirit; blue calms; pink is the color for love.

So strong are the vibrations of color that there is even a new healing art called color breathing, in which you visualize the energy field of a particular color, breathe it in—and see results.

Make use of the power of color! Dress your walls, your table, your lightbulbs, your bed, your shelves and your self according to what mood you want to bring out in yourself and induce in others.

Sensitize yourself to the power color already exerts over your mood. Using the rooms in your house and a friend's, or using the model rooms in an interiors showroom, observe yourself in markedly different colored surroundings: a very blue room, a very red-dominated one, a pink. Or among dark woody hues, then pale dusted ones, then clear bright primaries. What different thoughts go through your mind; what feelings fill your heart in each environment? How does your breathing, your posture, your level of tension or relaxation, your energy level differ? Think back on rooms that have strong mood associations for you— a room in your childhood house that you always felt blessedly secure and safe in; a room you've been in that gives you the jitters, makes you depressed, makes you wish it were your own. Did any of those rooms have a dominant color? What was it?

Next, sensitize yourself to your responsibility to that power. At no time more than in your intimate hours at home is your mood (and your loved ones' moods) so open to the power of color. Why? You're feeling more than thinking now; receiving rather than creating stimuli. Your emotional "vents" are wide open to whatever influence is presented. Make that influence a positive one.

Finally, sensitize yourself to your power over the wonderful power of color. At no other time and in no other place during your day do you have such fabulous control of the colors that surround you. Think about it. During your Public Self hours, you're in and out of street, cars, offices, stores. You don't control those color schemes. About the best you can hope for is control over the wall color, paintings, drapes and flowers in your office—which is only good enough to suffice, but not good enough to be glorious with. Also, your Public Self clothes are usually of darker, more practical colors than the colors that really make you feel marvelous (and look the most marvelous on you).

Dina Merrill

So the magic power of color is pretty well lost to you by day and in public.

But at home, at night, in your Intimate Self life, you've got that power in your own hands. Seize it! Play with it! Run with it!

First of all, understand that you have a preharmonized color palette to work with, for the colors that intimate wear come in more closely blend with the color of home furnishings and of cosmetics than do the colors of any other kind of clothing. (I get some of my best color ideas not from Paris couture shades of the moment but by walking past the eye makeup counters at department stores!) So with your coloring, your clothes, your flowers, your table settings, your furniture, fabrics and walls—even your food!—you have the makings of a marvelous, integrated palette with which to paint an original, exquisite, mood-making visual setting for your intimate hours.

Here are six wonderful palettes, each of which I visualize for you, depending on what part of the country you live in or have furnished your home to evoke. In almost all of them, I've started with the colors of nature, since these colors are literally the colors of life. And each is centered around some kind of party or gathering you might have—because the power of color, when you use it to its utmost, is too good not to be shared.

Let's start on my intimate color tour of America.

Visual #1: Tropical Dash

Think Florida, coastal Georgia and the Carolinas, the Caribbean, the Gulf Coast—and you think of one of the most distinctive color palettes in all of nature: coral, turquoise, fuschia, and emerald. These are strong colors, hot colors, bright colors—fun colors. Think of red haloconia, pink ginger and yellow hibiscus.

These are colors with dash and verve, all right, and I see you making the most of them at a very casual, open-air lunch or brunch, by pool or patio filled with the whitest of white wicker and ceramics.

Visual #5: Desert Drama

You live in Arizona, New Mexico, Utah, southern California or Texas. What wonderful drama you've got in sagebrush hues, dune color, cactus hues! Notice the brilliant sunset that surrounds you, and try to capture it. Joanna Carson says, "I love that magical moment when the sun goes down and I'm lighting the candles. Everything looks more beautiful bathed in candlelight."

I see you hostessing an outdoor barbeque at summer sundown amid desert flowers and blooming cactus in great clay pots. I see adobe pink, saddle leather and straw and clay colors everywhere, pierced by some objects in wonderful lacquered primaries—a bright blue vase here, a red lacquer tray there—peppering the toasty palette like dune wildflowers.

As for you, you've got on an Aztec or Peruvian woven fabric, a cropped top and mid-calf skirt edged with fringe in sunset colors, or maybe a bandeau top with a combination of different prints with an ankle-length cut culotte, with wooden bangle bracelets, wonderful big earrings of hammered gold and flat-heeled sandals that wrap around your ankle.

Joanna Carson

Visual #6: Pacific Northwest Splendor

If you live in the Pacific Northwest, I see you in a stone-and-glass house (whether private home or apartment) overlooking a babbling brook with giant firs. I see the interior spacious and sparse, with sleek, pure, comfortable shapes for the furniture, Oriental overtones in the accessories and dramatic sculptures—all silhouetted against the sunset. I see cherry blossom branches in Oriental urns, or curly willow branches complemented by one stalk of a vibrant red banana flower. I see a palette of beiges, fawns, stone grays that harmonize with the nature outside. I see the sofas, ottomans and floor cushions done in wonderful textures: nubby wools, slubbed silk and linens. And I see you, the hostess, spending a casual evening with friends in a marvelous pair of Chinese-inspired silk pajamas. In this setting you have many choices, because you are set against a neutral background. You would look good in bright colors or soft colors. One of my favorites is a deep, dramatic color such as indigo blue.

Once you start seeing your intimate life as a color visual hand-tailored by you, there's no stopping the beauty, the drama—the possibilities.

But color requires a bit—just a little—caution and balance. I give you the following hints in rhyme, so you'll remember them better (and because in fashion, all rules are meant to be broken, so don't take them terribly seriously):

<u>White's not always right.</u> The old wisdom to always wear a touch of white near your face isn't necessarily good advice. Yes, white is a positive color and it brings attention to your face. But for some of you pale-skinned blondes, white close to the face can make your hair look yellow (or, worse, make your teeth look yellow). Wear it carefully; look long and hard in the mirror, under a variety of lights, first.

<u>Cut fabric back with black.</u> The more black you wear, the more skin should show. And remember, you can wear an accent color with black

such as fuschia or electric blue. It's a strong, dark color; you've got to soften it, balance it, air it out, or else, from a distance, you'll look funereal, and that's probably not what you had in mind.

Black lace is good; backless black or strapless black is good; short black, for some, can be marvelous. And black and white is wonderful.

For rich or shiny fabrics, pale can prevail. Throughout history and in all cultures, pale, dusted colors have stood for refinement and high social status. After all, in the past only the most privileged could stay away from the dirtying toils of life, thus enabling them to wear pale and extravagant clothes.

Pale also means you have the kind of self-confidence and under-statement that come from good breeding. (When I was in India some years back, I marveled at the wonderfully bright colors in the streets of Delhi to my hostess, a maharani who was dressed in a pale-peach-and-gold-embroidered sari. "Ah, yes," she allowed, "but we don't wear those."

For this reason pale colors lend a certain class, restraint and balance to rich or shiny fabrics. Here are some of my favorite light colors: I think satin looks more expensive in soft dusted colors, and panné velvet looks richest in silver pearl gray or dusted pastels. I think polyester charmeuse is most beautiful in antique rose, hammered satin in light grape, silk or polyester jacquard in mauve.

Embrace your face. My first rule of thumb is: Be respectful of your own beauty. Wear colors, first of all, to flatter—to indulge, to honor, to be kind to—your face.

Keep the soft and life-giving colors—the "good" colors, I call them—near your face; the darker, muddier, industrial colors farther down. I won't design clothes with those colors near the face. A few years ago, when khaki green was all the rage, I used it sparingly, only in accents in a print and not near the face. I deal with charcoal by softening and lustering it into a light, silvery pearl gray trimmed with pink.

Redheads: Rethink pink. Pinks compete with your own natural coloring—your hair, your skin. But certain pinklike shades—mauves, lavenders, peaches or corals—look marvelous on a redhead. Rhonda Fleming and Rita Hayworth have looked great in them. Film Star Arlene Dahl's favorite color is mauve; even her stationery is mauve. Emerald or turquoise are also great colors for redheads, as well as cream and black. And I always include a little mauve as my signature color in every collection.

Blondes: Screen green. Yellowy greens are troublesome for blondes. Like some whites, they tend to bring out the yellow in hair, teeth, skin. However, dusty blue-green, jades and rose pinks can be good. Some blondes often look smashing in black; others, like Cheryl Ladd, look marvelous in a mixture of creams and beiges.

Brunettes: Bright is right. Pales are generally not as flattering on dark-haired women as bright colors: purple, red, electric blue, hot pink, bright turquoise, black and white. Experiment with those sharp, pure colors. Linda Gray does.

And, all you women:

It's your rainbow: Relish it! Run with it! Don't be afraid of color. Dare to make mistakes.

Walls can be repainted, couches recovered, furniture rearranged and clothes exchanged. Go by instinct. Listen to your fancy. There are color services available to help you travel through uncharted waters.

But don't take the spontaneity out of the process of looking at and choosing color. Embrace risk. Sometimes, in color as in all of life, mistakes lead to marvelous breakthroughs.

My earliest love affair with color started when Technicolor was introduced to the movie screen. I sat transfixed during *South Pacific;* those glorious island hues were magic to my Indiana eyes. Suffused with the pinkish and yellowish backlight, the "Bali Ha'i" scene seemed like a dream.

Well, I learned later that that very dreamlike backlight was a processing mistake in the developing of the film! An <u>accident</u> had created magic that changed my mood for the entire day and touched my life forever.

Risk the accidents. Relish the power of color. Use it for what it is: one of the prime energies for enticement.

I remember a wonderful story about Diana Vreeland, when she was editor-in-chief of *Vogue* magazine. The scene was her office, famous for its lacquered red walls and leopard carpet. She was like the queen bee, poised behind her desk, surrounded by all her protégés, who were most excited at the arrival of the new designs from the Paris collections. Hysteria began to set in as they all started to tear open the boxes, which were beautifully packed in every color of tissue paper. In all the confusion, someone accidentally dropped a burning cigarette ash. As the room went up in a blaze, most of the staff began to panic, pushing and shoving and running out of the office. But Mrs. Vreeland, being a Libra, the sign of balance, took it in stride. One editor saw her lean back, take a long draw on her cigarette and exclaim, "God, what color, color, color!" Needless to say, the next cover of *Vogue* featured a blaze of hot reds, fiery yellows and neon oranges.

That's certainly one way to take a risk with colors, but I hope that your encounters aren't quite so dangerous.

Chapter Seven

Ambience

Y ou've gotten yourself in the mood for enticement.

You've got your fabulous Intimate Self clothes on.

And you're using the power of color to help build just the right ambience for enticement.

Now what you need to make that ambience work for you is an atmosphere that absolutely pampers you . . . that heals and restores and rewards you.

Let's not forget what your day was like. You were girded in structured clothes. You were out and about on the concrete, in traffic jams, in harshly lit offices.

What you deserve now—what you <u>need</u> now—is to ensconce yourself in a temple of beauty and peace. And whether you live on a sumptuous estate with guest rooms to spare or in a studio apartment, you can create that temple in your own home.

Much of what I'm going to tell you, you already know. But you've forgotten about it. Or you do things for others, but not for yourself. Flowers, for example. <u>Never underestimate the power of fresh flowers in a room.</u> Although you may have been filling your living room with flowers for years, when was the last time you had a small bouquet of roses or violets near your bed? Or kept crushed rose petals or an exotic mixed potpourri at your bedside?

You've always arranged environments to please and pamper others—your husband, your children, your guests and your friends. Now it's time to arrange your environment to please and pamper you.

Let's not forget light. Make light caress you, be your lover and your friend. Suffuse your rooms with soft lighting, the kind that makes the room glow and reflects the colors in it. Keep intimate nighttime lighting shaded, recessed or indirect, and never underestimate the power of candles.

And, above all, think intimacy. Mario Buatta, the New York decorator, says, "I like the chairs and couches in a room to talk to one another. The first thing I do when I'm designing is to put the seating face to face and see what the pieces 'say.'"

Beds and bedrooms have always sent powerful messages, throughout time. During the Middle Ages and the Renaissance, while the peasantry slept ten to a room on scratchy straw, fifteenth-century French royalty flaunted their power by holding court in huge bedrooms on gigantic beds. Those beds got even bigger throughout the sixteenth century and the seventeenth, until the French Revolution cut them down to size (along with their inhabitants' heads).

In the twentieth century the movies played up the bedroom's erotic power. When Carroll Baker played Jean Harlow, for example, she was ensconced in a round, peach-color bedroom the size of a presidential suite, and a big round bed was platformed like a shrine to sensuality. Occasionally movie censors (especially in the fifties) promoted the use of separate beds, but nobody was fooled.

Today beds run the gamut from the highly romantic, private, canopied style to the very sleek platform, with many points in between.

According to Mario Buatta, "the ultimate bed is canopied, making you want to climb right in and get comfortable. It's hung with gauze or tambour (embroidered cotton fabric from Switzerland or Ireland), so you're looking out at the world as if through a fine, cloudy film of mist. It's lit softly, indirectly, with pink light. Fur rugs are on each side, so your feet aren't cold when you step down. And everything in and around it is fresh, clean and fragrant."

Some women worry that canopied beds are too feminine for their husbands to be comfortable in."Yes, they are feminine," Buatta says. "Sometimes a husband will protest his wife's decision. But once he gets into that canopied bed, he never wants to get out!"

And <u>that</u> is what you want.

Mostly, though, you want to feel pampered.

Let beauty surround you and entice you. I've made a list of my favorite ways to do this.

Twelve Sensual Suggestions for Pampering Yourself

1. <u>Dress your bed with beautiful linens</u>—hand-embroidered pillow cases, antique sheets, satin sheets. Remember, your body is going to spend eight of its most intimate, unguarded hours caressed by those sheets; make them glorious enough to invite the mind to wonderful dreams and massage the skin to the rest it deserves. And spray those sheets with perfume before you get between them!

2. On top of those sheets <u>throw a soft, wonderful duvet</u> (one of those large, marvelous European down-filled comforters). The duvet might be cotton on one side, silk or satin on the other. Or it could be all cotton—try a white-on-white jacquard cotton with hand embroidery.

3. <u>Don't forget to indulge your sense of smell.</u> If it's a beautiful spring night, take fresh spring flowers and buy matching oils for your potpourri

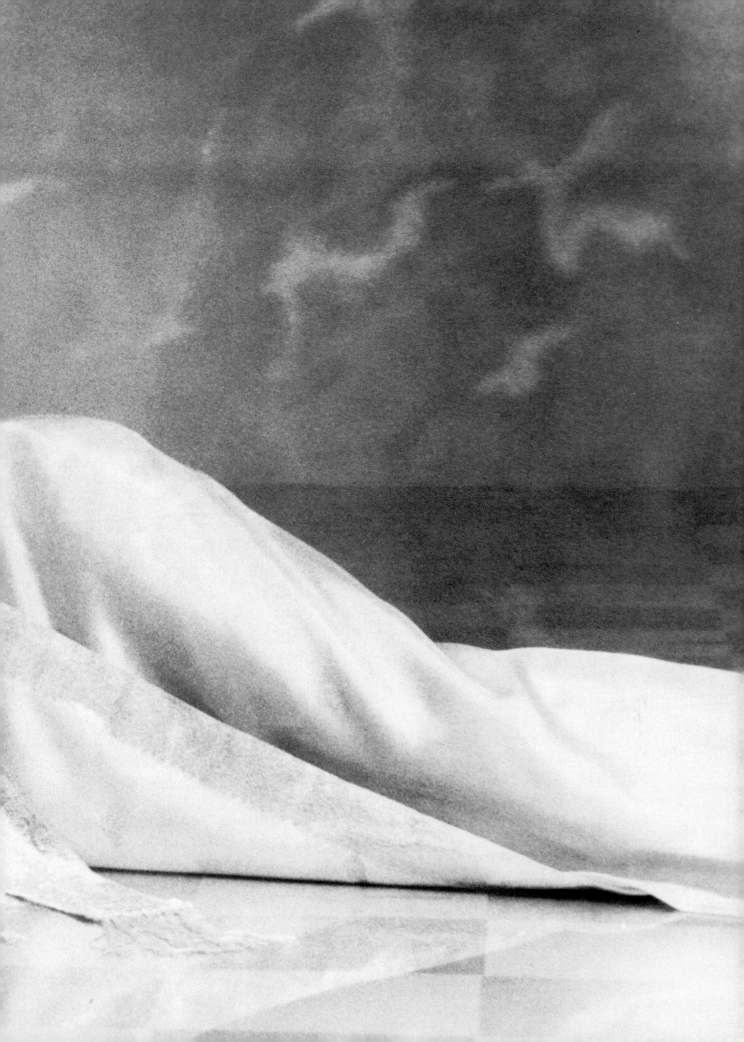

or scented light bulb rings. And put wonderful assorted sachets in your lingerie drawers.

4. <u>The mind needs beauty, too.</u> Read something beautiful before you go to bed—such as Keats or Browning for romance. Read anything that makes you want to take the book into your dream. And this also means . . .

5. <u>Set your mind at rest by writing down those thoughts you're afraid of losing.</u> I used to slip into sleep trying to "hold on" to a design that had just come to me. I was so fearful of losing it that I could hardly go to sleep at all. Then I started leaving a pad and pencil near my bed so I could draw the design—and sink into glorious, untroubled sleep. You can do the same with your thoughts. Buy the prettiest velvet or fine leather-backed pad and a slender, delicate pen, or if your taste runs high-tech, try a tape recorder. And use them for last-minute presleep thoughts so that you can go to your slumper without the slightest bit of tension.

6. <u>Pamper your tired feet, too.</u> Have a variety of beautiful, comfortable bed slippers to make you feel pampered from the soles of your feet on up. Try slippers of satin, lace or maybe embroidered velvet. Or you might wear all-out-sexy high-heeled slippers touched with maribou.

7. <u>If you travel a lot, personalize—and beautify—your hotel room.</u> Well-known author and lecturer Arianna Stassinopoulos always travels with what she calls her "Aphrodite traveling kit." In it she carries perfumed candles for the bedroom and bathroom, her current favorite piece of lingerie and very thin chiffon scarves that she drapes over the hotel-room paintings ("I don't know why," she laughs, "but most hotel-room paintings are real eyesores!"). She also always carries with her a small cassette recorder and her favorite classical and contemporary music, including music to exercise to.

Bring some beautiful pictures of loved ones. Have fragrant fresh flowers delivered to your room, and slip into your favorite travel robe. Audrey Hepburn even used to bring her own china and linens to hotels.

8. If you're building a new house, don't put a fireplace only in the

128

living room. <u>Nothing's so marvelous as a hearth and a fire right at the foot of your bed.</u>

9. And speaking of building drama and romance into a house . . . Friends of mine built a very modern home in the desert. They <u>put in a skylight directly over the bed</u>. At night, whenever they wish, they just push a button and the ceiling rolls back, revealing an expanse of heavenly stars for them to sleep and dream under.

10. Why not a bathroom built for two? Install a sunken marble tub and serve him a cocktail there every night!

11. <u>By all means embrace the sensual myths of past cultures.</u> A friend of mine has a statue of an Indian goddess of love in her bedroom. I don't know if it helps, but she swears by it! Throughout recorded history the swan, the fish and the dove have symbolized soft, compassionate womanhood in many cultures.

12. <u>Don't forget mirrors.</u> They're wonderful in the bedroom, dressing room and bath because they reflect dreams and fantasies. I have been in the business of selling dreams all my life, and often the illusion is more important than the reality. Mirrors tell the truth. Your back is as important as your front. Let your mirror be your guide to beauty and a more beautiful you.

Put them all together—feast in the sensuality of the environment, and let yourself be gloriously enticed . . . and enticing.

Chapter Eight

Living Out Enticement

W e've seen how important clothes, the bath, the mood, colors and the environment are to the dance of intimacy. Still, all that is embellishment—atmosphere—accessory.

The <u>real</u> stuff of the dance of intimacy is its performance. That performance can be ordinary, or it can be dazzling.

I'm only interested in the dazzling. I don't want the clothes I design or the women who wear them to settle for anything less. How can you make sure you don't?

Come. Let me show you how to look at intimate clothes in such a way that pure dazzle is what you get from the dance of intimacy.

Here are some of the questions you should ask when you are about to make your purchase that will assure you of making the right choice:

• Does this undergarment (bra, panty, teddy, slip) make me feel I'm hiding a wonderful sensual secret self under my practical daytime clothes?

• Does the feel of my intimate wear tingle and caress my own skin, sending messages to my nerve endings that put me in a sensual mood?

• And does that same fabric induce the hand of another to keep softly, slowly touching it, then move on to the skin underneath?

• Does this garment slip off my body in one sinuous glide so that I look and feel like an elegantly disrobing goddess? Does it allow me to undress (or him to undress me) without either of us breaking touch, eye contact or stride?

Together, in private now, let's ask those questions of your intimate wear. Let's get right down to it and analyze the actual enticeability of your new wardrobe. And in doing so, let's explore . . .

Secrets, Lure and Touch:
The Three Magic Powers of Intimate Clothes

Picture your intimate clothes in three stages in three different time frames during the day. First, during your Public Self life, you wear undergarments hidden beneath your clothes, experienced only by you, full of the power of <u>secrets</u>.

This is the power of your undergarments to make you feel you're hiding something spicy and special—your secret self, the other side of your moon—from someone who, if he's lucky, might glimpse it, and—if he's really lucky—might touch it.

Secrets make you feel that the other person is lucky to be near you. And that's the most advantageous power of all in a blossoming intimacy.

Secrets also mean luxury. To have something beautiful and to display it for all the world to see: that's nice . . . but it's also obvious. But to have something beautiful and to <u>conceal</u> it—to relish it secretly, alone—<u>that's</u> a great privilege.

These secrets are your own personal, close-to-the-skin prelude to the mood you want to give yourself to at the end of your busy day.

And when you get to the end of that day and to your Intimate Self, you also get to the power to <u>lure</u>.

Now you're home. You want to be wearing intimate clothes that will lure your partner to intimacy, whether the merely emotional kind or the physical. You want clothes that send a message to the man who looks at you—and at them. That message may be: "Trust me; confide in me; relax with me." Or it may be: "Come close to me. Be excited by me."

When clothes have the power to lure, they have the power to activate the male heart, imagination and pulse. They can convince an ordinary, perhaps preoccupied, home-from-work husband to scuttle his evening's plan for the sake of romance.

Clothes that have the power to lure wipe out the ordinary and replace it with the spectacular: the suggestion of heightened gratifications to come, moments—or seconds—from now.

And that time gap—that sense of wishful waiting—means that, as well, lure is expectation. Clothes with the power to lure are clothes that subtly play with time, that tease a tiny bit. Clothes with the power to lure demand that your partner <u>wait</u>. (He <u>wants</u> to wait; it makes it all the more exciting!)

Now, let's move on to the power of <u>touch</u>. Touch is contact by stages: hand to fabric, skin to fabric, skin to skin. It's the sweet, sure dance of two softly clothed bodies experiencing one another. A garment's power of touch, then, relies heavily on the grace with which it can be shed.

Let me tell you how the clothes you choose, wear and delight in have the three magical powers of intimacy. First, there's <u>the power of secrets.</u>

In Elizabethan times in England, women wore three petticoats to hold out their dresses. The topmost one was called the modest one; the middle one was called the mischievous one; and the one closest to the body was called the secret one. That one was the most special because it was the closest to the skin. Today, of course, we dress in fewer layers; our "secret" and "mischievous" selves are one.

If you're practical and work-oriented during your Public Self day, why not keep the marvelous secret of your true sensuality close to your skin, where no one but you knows it's there? Wear the laciest black panties, bra and slip under a black wool business suit . . . satin panties under tweeds (I love that combination of textures). The result? A psychological lift that translates to grand self-confidence.

"Too much practical lingerie makes a dull woman," warned a 1932 issue of *Vogue*. "An occasional frill is good for the soul." I heartily agree!

But do be careful. Don't spoil your secret with gaucherie. For example:

• Never wear dark underwear (no matter how beautiful) under a light or sheer blouse or dress. Nothing looks more inappropriate than a woman walking down the street in a light-colored blouse, the outline of her black bra showing through. However, this is not true with light underwear and dark clothes. White is always right. Try a beautiful white satin camisole and tap pants under your dark business suit.

• Never wear an undergarment that doesn't fit properly, no matter how beautiful it is.

• Try underthings in beautiful, refined pastel colors. Pale colors are much more flattering to your skin and more workable in your wardrobe, and they look more expensive. Try:

> very soft ivory with ecru lace
> delicate mauve with either ecru or matching lace
> beautiful violet blue
> powered peach
> beautiful champagne

• For a change of pace be a little daring and try bright lemon yellow cotton panties and bra. Or maybe a luscious crimson red satin teddy or tap pant and camisole.

• If you're going straight from day to romance, with no time to switch to your Intimate Self clothes, build your clothes from the skin out and wear:

> a pale cocoa silk bra, panties and slip under brown or beige tweedy office clothes
> platinum silver satin underwear under a gray flannel suit

• And don't forget to perfume yourself where skin meets elastic.

You can never underestimate the power of silk on a woman's skin. The vast majority of women never wear it. Broadway producer Flo Ziegfeld, when asked why he spent so much money on silk underwear for his famous Ziegfeld girls, replied, "Obviously you don't understand women and the psychological power of silk next to their bodies."

Beautiful lingerie like this tells a man, "Here is a woman who cares about herself, who respects herself right down to all the details, who treats her body with quality—and who therefore must expect quality treatment from others." You must care about yourself enough to take the time and effort to achieve your best secret self.

And don't forget, too:

• Many women wear cotton underwear because they love the feel on hot sticky summer days. It breathes and keeps you cool, even in the heat of summer as no man-made fiber can. Still, you want it to look beautiful. Why not trim that cotton panty with French lace or delicate embroidery?

• In summer, too, with less layered outer clothes, make sure your underwear doesn't show through. Teddies have the advantage over panties, bras and slips of fewer layers and no elastic.

• Tap pants are marvelous—but be careful to wear them under a full skirt. If you put a jersey or another knitted, body-grazing fabric over a tap pant, the outlines of the pant will show through.

Finally, of course, the most fabulous secrets are always meant to be, ever so elegantly, betrayed. So:

• Let your secret show! A pure silk embroidered camisole peeking out from under a waist-tied blouse is beautiful. One of my favorite looks is a cinnamon or champagne silk camisole under a black velvet dinner suit, with black onyx and diamond clips.

Speaking of possibilities, let's move now to the next time stage of intimacy: the point at which, home after a Public Self day, you're ready to put on clothes to help you attain <u>the power to lure.</u>

Luring is a beautiful ceremony—a deft, calculated choreography of seduction.

It's baited breath . . . heightened heartbeat . . . speeded pulse . . . appetite teased and whetted by slight delays . . . imagination spurred by what is hidden and what is suggested and what is only partially shown.

<u>Lure:</u> the wonderful, sensual, slow tug of the word and the force—this is what men love in a woman . . . and in her intimate clothes. For men, all the fun of the game of romance—all the challenge—is ruined when there are no hurdles to overcome. Couples in the Middle Ages may have signaled a readiness for lovemaking to one another by going to bed completely nude (so much so that a bad promise in business was described by saying, "A promise like that is as much good as a married woman who would go to bed in a nightshirt!"). But we've progressed quite a bit from those days.

For the past several centuries men have felt, well, frankly deprived if their objects of desire were too readily revealed. It is thought that nightgowns got longer in the thirties because street clothes for women got shorter. (Shapely legs that were seen freely by day were much more compelling if they were suddenly hidden at night, moments before lovemaking.) But perhaps the best words on the subject were written by an anonymous eighteenth-century poet:

> At times to veil is to reveal
> And to display is to conceal;
> The vision's finer than the view;
> [A woman's] landscape Nature never drew
> So fair as fancy draws

One of the most beautiful examples of this power to lure that I've ever seen was the seduction scene in a movie of a few years ago, *The Other Side of Midnight*. In it a famous actress, portrayed by Marie-France Pisier, is being wooed by a Greek billionaire. He is dying to have her, and she decides to seduce him with the artful, elegant gradualness that he wants.

He invites her to his island villa. There, each night, he sends her a fabulous gift: a diamond-and-sapphire ring . . . a pair of diamond drop earrings . . . a ruby-and-diamond necklace. The maid brings her each offering, and the woman turns down each one.

Then, on the fourth night, the maid brings the woman a single long-stemmed red rose on a satin pillow. <u>That's</u> the night she knows she's got him.

She gets up, walks down the hall, throws open the big double doors to his bedroom suite and stands before him. She takes out her hair combs and shakes her head. Her hair tumbles down in shimmering cascades.

Then, with a single pull at her shoulder, her sheer toga glides down over her body: the body he's longed to possess all this time. The toga falls to the floor.

You can <u>feel</u> the pull of the lure, as if it were a highly charged magnet.

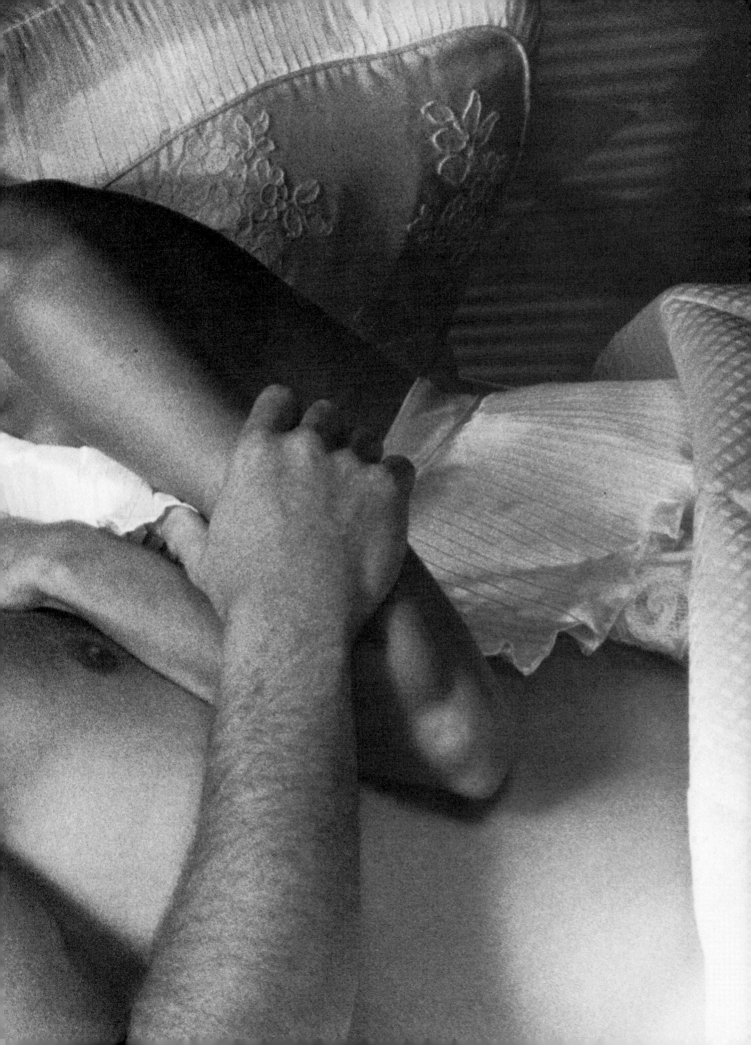

That scene brings together all four of what I think are the powerful components of the power of lure: (1) <u>elusiveness</u> (the woman kept eluding her host's overtures by sending back his gifts and remaining aloof to his advances); (2) <u>subtlety, understatement and metaphor</u> (the rose makes the erotic point far better than the expensive jewelry—believe me, she'll get those diamonds later. And the rose brings out his sensitivity and sexuality); (3) <u>heightened anticipation</u> (both parties waited until tension and desire had reached the near-breaking point); and (4) <u>the glorious, theatrical, all-in-one-sweep abandonment of clothing</u> (the sweep of silk caressing the body).

The right intimate clothes can help give you the glorious power to lure in all these four ways. In fact, some intimate clothes contain that power <u>within</u> them. Which of them do? Let's see.

Nine Enticing Looks

1. <u>A beautiful lace robe or a total-lace bed jacket</u> is very provocative. Here is elusiveness in peak form (the skin is hinted at through the lace). And lace (especially if it's white) symbolizes virtue and innocence.

2. For a subtler way of making the same statement, try a <u>gown, teddy or sleep shirt of georgette with satin stripes or patterns.</u> The georgette provides the bit of see-through; the satin heightens that effect with high-sheen, touch-compelling sophistication. Or try a garment that is part-opaque, part semi-sheer, in cotton, chiffon or satin.

3. A wonderful <u>long robe with sheer sleeves</u>, through which you can see the bareness of the arms under a sheer screen, is marvelous. A design I created a few seasons ago is a purple satin kimono with long, purple chiffon butterfly sleeves, edged in matching satin, with a stitched obi belt. It was quite enticing.

4. A long, loose, floor-length <u>poet's shirt</u> in pristine embroidered white cotton batiste is wonderful for subtlety and understatement. The fabric; the color; the soft, blousy sleeves with lots of shirring: all this suggests decorum and reserve that send an irresistible message.

5. A beautiful <u>gown with the back exposed</u> draws a man's eye when you ever so subtly turn around. For absolute drop-dead lure, it could be a <u>bias-cut gown</u> (so each curve and rounding of the body is hugged and suggested) of a fabulously liquid material: hammered satin, silk-satin, charmeuse. These materials catch and reflect light; they make you shimmer; they invite the hand. They're quite irresistible.

And they make it very clear that <u>you're</u> painting the picture, <u>you're</u> directing the movie. He will respond by playing whatever role you write for him. So if you go backless, his eyes will go right to your back. If you wear something short—a sleep shirt, teddy, camisole and tap pant—his eye will go to your legs. The marvelous balance between clothed and unclothed is what you are creating. As you dress for these nights, be deliciously aware of your power to stage the evening according to the kinds of attention and touch you want.

6. Be aware of the dramatic possibilities in your night wear. <u>Kimonos and wrap robes</u> (the slinkier and more liquid the material, the better) can be dropped with one grand sensual sweep of hand on sash. How much more full of impact than buttoned or zippered robes.

7. By the same token, <u>tap pants, teddies, camisoles and sleep chemises</u> have a wonderful insouciance written right in. Wearing them, you look as if you can, with one step and one hand fling, get right out of these little nothings, as if they were mere hankies.

8. As the heroine of *The Other Side of Midnight* knew, there's nothing like the <u>one-shouldered toga</u>. One brisk flick at the shoulder and it slides gorgeously down the body.

9. Still, there are times when you want to project not ease of undress but its opposite—the romance, the extraordinary heightened anticipation. When you want that, try a three-quarter-length satin coat or kimono over a beautiful black camisole and black satin pajamas. Everything drops off in layers: coat/kimono . . . camisole . . . pants. The wonderful sheen and feel of the satin caresses the skin (yours and his) and looks very luxurious.

Which brings us to <u>the power of touch</u>. Panné velvet is one of my favorite fabrics: it's tactile, comforting, sensual, and irresistible. For that special evening, try a panné velvet robe with nothing underneath but perfume, or with a bias silk-satin slip gown, or a wisp of a teddy.

And while you're thinking of the utter pleasure of touch . . .

- <u>Think feathers!</u> Imagine a beautiful black ostrich jacket tipped in white over a black silk gown. But remember I love feathers; you have to love them, too, for them to work their magic.

- <u>Watch out for georgettes and chiffons.</u> They're lovely, yes—but make sure they're not too stiff or too scratchy.

- Go with some of the new fabrics that have <u>satin on the outside, brushed flannel on the inside.</u> The more caressed your skin feels by your garment, the more enticing you'll feel.

- <u>Soft cottons</u> have become year-round fabrics. They're pure, they're washable and they soften with age.

- <u>Cotton and polyester jerseys</u> feel marvelous to the hand and to the skin. They're light, they drape beautifully and they soften the female figure.

Do a whole-hand touch test on a gown you're considering buying. Close your eyes and, in the privacy of the fitting room, feel it against your bare skin. Is the whole effect pleasing? Does the fabric's feel seem to invite the hand to keep touching? Look and feel for objects that might hurt the body—buttons particularly, and zippers. God knows you don't want a casualty!

Throughout the centuries special healers have found the greatest capacity for soothing, curing and uplifting the spirit in the hands. Those "healers' hands" are yours as well. Cherish the fact, and use them well. "The greatest sense in our body is our touch sense," said J. Lionel Tiger in *The Stages of Human Life.* "It is probably the chief sense in the processes of sleeping and waking; it gives us our knowledge of depth or thickness and form; we feel, we love and hate, are touchy and are touched, through the touch corpuscles of our skin."

We feel—and create and give—enticement through that touch, that skin, as well.

Enticement, you see, goes way beyond clothes—to the skin, to the heart, to the spirit. Take your best possible self and soar!

A Parting Note

Have you enjoyed the time we've spent together? I hope so. I wanted it to be fun.

I also want it to help you, and I can't help but feel that it has. "Live and let live" may be the motto of some. But "Live and help live" is a motto of mine.

I don't expect you to take all of my advice. What I hope I've given you is a new vision of what you owe yourself at day's end and of what you deserve to feel like and deserve to be.

I want you to be left with that image, that dazzling possibility, and to take that image and incorporate it into your life. Even if you apply only a few of these ideas to your real life tomorrow, you will have made a good start.

<u>Enticement.</u> Think enticement and then relax; let the meaning of the word, the clothes, the fantasy and the allure awaken in your heart and transfer your intimate life. As Ralph Waldo Emerson says, "It is easy to live for others; everybody does. I call on you to live for yourselves."

Bill Tice